THE 10 PRINCIPLES OF A

LOVE

Based Culture

HOW AUTHENTIC BUSINESS
LEADERS TRUST THEIR EMPLOYEES
TO DO THE RIGHT THING

WRITTEN BY ENTREPRENEUR

IVO NELSON

with Dana Sellers

10 Principles of a Love-Based Culture

ISBN   978-1-7337632-0-2   (Trade paper)
ISBN   978-1-7337632-1-9   (Hard cover)
ISBN   978-1-7337632-2-6   (Ebook)

Editing: Jessica Hatch, Hatch Editorial Services
Book design and production: Becky's Graphic Design
Cover design: Becky's Graphic Design
Illustrations: Becky Bayne and Kayla Swedberg

Printed and bound in USA
First printing April 2019

Published by IVO
967 Interstate 45 South, Huntsville, Texas 77340
www.lovebasedculture.com
For ordering information please email marketing@ivo.com

Dedicated to my dad, Ivo A. Nelson

Ivo's Love-Based Family
My wife, Sally
Our children Erik, Azi, Ashley and Ryan
Our grandkids Aiden, Dolores, and Calvin

Dana's Love-Based Family
My husband, Gene
Our children Lamar and Karalisa, Baine and Sara
Our grandkids Crockett and Houston

CONTENTS

Foreword		vii
Introduction		xi
1	100% Referenceability	1
2	Leadership	21
3	Core Values	47
4	A Higher Calling	65
5	Governance	83
6	Compensation	105
7	Winning	127
8	The Three Ps	147
9	Decision-Making	165
10	Acts of Love	187
11	A Final Call to Action	201
	Notes	213
	Bibliography	219
	Acknowledgments	223
	Join the Conversation	227

FOREWORD

When I first met Ivo, he had a stern black mustache and a very impatient attitude. Ivo and I were pioneers in the early days of healthcare information technology, trying to do things that had never been done before. He had been tasked with starting up Zale Lipshy University Hospital in Dallas, Texas, as the first fully automated hospital, the "Hospital of the Future," and two healthcare applications from the company I had cofounded, Trinity Computing Systems, had been chosen for use at Zale.

We next crossed paths a few years later, when we were reintroduced by Ivo's wife, Sally.

Thanks to that meeting, in 1992, I joined Ivo and a handful of others who were starting a healthcare information technology consulting firm that came to be known as Healthlink. Little did I know that Ivo and I were destined to work together for most of our professional lives.

Over the years, Ivo's stern black mustache has come and gone (and come back again with a few gray hairs mixed in), but his attitude of impatience hasn't changed. From the very beginning, Ivo and I were each other's yin and yang. Ivo was (and still is) a brilliant visionary who knew where we needed to go, and he demanded we get there fast! I was more analytical in my approach. Over time, we developed a trusting relationship: I trusted Ivo's intuitive decisions, and he respected my ability to execute them.

While Ivo and I were completely different in our management styles, we were always totally aligned in our core values. We had a mantra that we passed on to all of our managers when they asked for direction on touchy situations: "Do the right thing." We all knew that "right" referred to what was best for our customers, regardless of the impact it would have on the company's bottom line. "Right" also showed respect for our employees' integrity and let them know we had their backs. When it came to ethics and doing what was "right," there was no gray area. Deep in our hearts, we knew that our customers were the only ones who could measure our success. It took all of us working together as a team to make them happy.

After Healthlink was acquired by IBM, Ivo and I moved on to the next phases of our professional lives. Ivo became an investor in and board member of numerous companies and stayed active with healthcare nonprofit organizations. I started Encore Health Resources, where Ivo was both an investor and a mentor. At Encore, my partners and I applied the same culture and leadership principles that we had used at Healthlink, again with amazing results. This led Encore to be ranked as one of the Best Places to Work in Healthcare by *Modern Healthcare* Magazine each year until its acquisition by Quintiles in 2014. Encore took fewer than five years to approach $100 million in annual revenue.

About a year after I retired, I got a call from Ivo, who said he wanted me to work with him on a book about our time at Healthlink. I said, "No way!" I was having too much fun spending time with my granddaughter, traveling, reading, and relaxing.

But Ivo was convinced we had something important to say, and his enthusiasm was contagious. As we talked about our experiences, we couldn't deny that what we had accomplished at Healthlink was something special. We also knew that it was replicable, as my experience with Encore had shown. I couldn't ignore Ivo's desire to teach those principles to others with the goal of improving both company finances and the lives of workers who had vastly different relationships with their jobs than we had enjoyed.

In *Love-Based Culture*, Ivo has captured the key elements that make up a love-based business. I add commentary on certain topics, which appear in italics throughout the chapters.

Whether you are an entrepreneur, just starting your career, or a team member at a Fortune 500 company, you will see your world change if you apply the concepts in this book to your life.

With much love and best wishes for your love-based journey,

Dana Sellers,
Former President and Chief Operating Officer, Healthlink

INTRODUCTION:

What is Love?

"Love" isn't a word much used in business. Some people may see the word "love" in the title of this book and visualize a bunch of hippies sitting around in a circle singing "Kumbaya" while their customers look elsewhere for products and services. The reality is quite different.

My first experience with love-based leadership came at a pivotal time, when I was in my early 20s and had dropped out of school. I had moved to the San Francisco Bay Area with no money and no skills. Needing to find some way to make a living, I decided to use the limited skills I possessed to start a handyman service. I placed an ad in a Palo Alto newspaper that read: "Handyman, $10/hr." Simple, but it hit on a great need. Soon, I got more work than I could handle. After taking a lot of one-off jobs, I found myself working for one of the big telecom companies in the area. This ended up dominating so much of my time that I accepted a job on their staff.

About a year later, while I was running the company's print shop, someone from HR came in with a stack of papers to be copied. I noticed that it was a list of every employee's salary.

I couldn't help but skim through. At the top, as you might expect, was the CEO, and at the bottom of this very long list was me. I was the lowest-paid person in the company. That didn't bother me; I was happy to have a job so that I could eat. Despite being the lowest-paid person at the company, I set the bar high for the work I did, going the extra mile to do my best when called upon to provide any service.

One day, I got a call from the CEO's secretary. Mr. Zelcovich wanted to schedule a meeting. This scared the crap out of me! Why would the top brass want to talk to me, the lowest-paid guy at his company?

I went up to his floor and was escorted into a private conference room, which seemed as large as a football field. Mr. Zelcovich walked in, sat down, and said, "Ivo, what are you doing with your life?"

This caught me off guard.

"Well, sir," I started to respond, "I'm running the print shop and doing okay," but he cut me off.

"Ivo, let me tell you what you're doing with your life. You're wasting it." He didn't give me a chance to reply. "You've got a reputation around here for the quality of work that you do. You work hard and everybody likes you. So here's what you need to do."

He then proceeded to lay out an unbelievable plan for my life. "You need to go back to college, get a technical degree, and then an MBA. After that, get a job with a company that has an excellent training program so you can learn. Spend at least five years there, and then you can decide whether to stay, move on to another company where you'll make more money, or start your own business."

The entire discussion lasted 15 minutes. I walked out of his office feeling like I had just met with God. I swear I could hear angels singing in the background.

Those 15 minutes changed my life. You really have to wrap your head around the fact that the CEO took time out of his schedule to help his lowest-paid employee. He showed me an Act of Love by letting me know that he cared about me.

That was more than 35 years ago, but I have never forgotten his generosity.

I listened to Mr. Zelcovich's advice. I packed my bags, moved back to Texas, and earned an information sciences degree from Baylor University. Then I joined a company that had a great training program in systems engineering, Electronic Data Systems (EDS), which was founded by Ross Perot and run by Mort Meyerson. I spent seven years at EDS and then helped Mr. Perot and other EDS executives start Perot Systems, where I ultimately ran operations for the healthcare division. Four years later, in 1992, I joined Insource Management Group (IMG), a company that we later renamed Healthlink. It succeeded because of the principles I learned from Mr. Zelcovich and others, who taught me that caring about people was not only good for employees, it was also good for business.

HIGH EMPLOYEE SATISFACTION LEADS TO BETTER COMPANY PERFORMANCE

Common sense tells you that a culture in which people like their jobs, like their bosses (at least most of the time), and love operating in the spirit of teamwork with their peers is going to result in happy, healthy, and prosperous people.

If you don't believe me, look at this finding from a 2018 study of corporate performance by the Drucker Institute: "[A] company's results are driven, to a major degree, by how well it manages its workforce."[1] Furthermore, of the 37 categories evaluated by the Institute to arrive at its Management Top 250, an annual ranking of corporate performance, "the employee category is the key source of change in total effectiveness scores over time."[2]

The companies listed in the Drucker Institute's Management Top 250 are "the highest scorers among 608 U.S. corporations studied that in the fall of 2016 belonged either to the S&P 500 stock index or Fortune 500 list or had a market value of more than $10 billion."[3] The 50 largest gainers improved by an average of 11.2% in employee engagement and development, while the 50 largest losers decreased in that category by an average of 13.2%.[4]

The World Economic Forum tackled the question of worker satisfaction and corporate social responsibility in 2015, when researcher Alex Edmans, professor of finance at the Wharton School of the University of Pennsylvania, presented his article, "Why Happier Workers Matter More than You Think."[5]

His research question—"Does corporate social responsibility improve the value of a company?"—continues to reverberate throughout all levels of business as companies worldwide reevaluate themselves.

> "Today, countless studies acknowledge the link between culture, trust, and business success."
> MICHAEL BUSH AND SARAH LEWIS-KULIN.

Edmans used the field of finance to investigate the long-standing management question of employee satisfaction. He went back to 1984, when the first "100 Best Companies to Work for in America"[6] list was published, and analyzed answers to 57 different questions on employee satisfaction.

When he compared the returns of the best companies to the overall market, as well as to companies in the same industry, he found that the best companies beat the market by 2 to 3% per year over the 25-year period from 1984 to 2009. These results suggest that employee satisfaction is beneficial to company value. Edmans writes, "Human capital is the main asset in many firms, and employee welfare can improve productivity, retention and recruitment."[7]

Similarly, the companies that make *Fortune* magazine's list of the "100 Best Companies to Work For" all have something in common. In 1997, when the list was first developed, "only the most forward-thinking business leaders appreciated the concrete value of creating employee-friendly workplaces." That has certainly changed. "Today, countless studies acknowledge the link between culture, trust, and business success."[8]

These studies are just a handful of many that validate the economic value of a healthy corporate culture. Most of you don't need studies to explain why a love-based culture would motivate you and your employees to deliver services or products with excellence. I believe that most leaders are inclined to operate on the basis of love but have been conditioned over the years, from their own experiences in fear-based office cultures, to manage from a place of fear. If something doesn't always feel quite right, it's because it isn't.

SO, WHAT IS LOVE IN BUSINESS?

In a professional setting, a love-based culture encourages its employees to look at their work as more than a function pigeonholed inside the tight confines of a job description. Instead, it encourages them to support the company's goals and to grow within their own capabilities. This empowers them with a "do whatever it takes" attitude that makes customers happy and the company successful. As a result, employees go the extra mile to do what is right for their company because they believe in the company, trust their colleagues, and respect their customers.

> ## "If you want to go quickly, you can go alone. If you want to go far, you must go together."
> AFRICAN PROVERB

It should be noted that a love-based culture applies both to how you relate to your employees, supervisors, and peers (*internal* love-based culture) as well as to how you relate to your customers, whether directly or indirectly through employees (*external* love-based culture). This will become especially clear in the first chapter, which discusses the love-based principle of 100% "referenceability."

In a love-based culture:

» Employees are encouraged to speak up when things aren't working and acknowledge issues EARLY if a project is in trouble. This gives the team plenty of time to jump in and fix it.

» A team is focused on achieving a common goal, and everyone knows their teammates have their backs.

» Leaders not only strive for collaboration and feedback, they also truly listen.

» Everyone believes in the company's core values and operates according to them.

» Team members are empowered to make decisions on behalf of their customers and don't need to ask for permission to do so.

» The lack of traditional hierarchy creates a level playing field, and everyone feels respected for the role they play in the company.

» Team members don't think twice about whether they're going to get paid more for helping. When someone on the team needs help, all you see are arms and legs flying to make it happen. This attitude and the ensuing results can't be measured, but are just as crucial to the health of the company as a balance sheet in the black.

» Everyone understands that not all performance can be measured in traditional ways. Ultimately, performance is the subjective opinion of a manager and therefore requires trust between the team member and their manager.

» People aren't nervous when their boss calls them into their office because they have shared trust. In a relationship of trust, employees know that their managers are looking out for their best interests. In such a relationship, a boss is more likely to help you reach the next level in your career than to criticize you.

» Failure and mistakes are learning opportunities. In an instance of failure, management circles the wagons to help with recovery and then explores the lessons learned, which are shared with everyone impacted. Everyone walks away smarter and better equipped to handle the situation should it arise again. Truly understanding the mistakes made and, more importantly, why they happened makes it far less likely that the same actions will be repeated in the future.

» Great ideas can blossom in an environment in which employees have no fear of retribution when they have a better idea than their boss.

» Employees are willing to spend time supporting what is traditionally considered "overhead" during their free time. While the company still needs to bear the brunt of the cost for time spent away from otherwise productive customer activities, people will invest their own time for the greater good.

» Employees look forward to going to work everyday because they believe in the company's mission and feel good about the work that they do.

» The ultimate goal of a love-based culture is "we."

Is it a stretch to call the behaviors listed above love? I don't think so.

Mr. Zelcovich wasn't the only person who taught me that love is not inconsistent with business. Another mentor was Ross Perot, the same man who ran for president in 1992 and rescued two EDS employees from an Iranian prison. Ross Perot, whom I was privileged to work for at EDS and at Perot Systems, was not only a savvy businessman but also a remarkably caring human being who demonstrated many Acts of Love, moments in which an individual is positively impacted by another, for his employees.

"Kindness is contagious, as is fear."
ANONYMOUS

One day when I was working at Perot Systems, an employee told me about his cancer diagnosis. Mr. Perot always wanted to know when someone had health issues, so I let him know immediately. His reaction was one of the most significant examples I have ever seen of a manager showing an Act of Love for an employee.

First, Mr. Perot made sure that this team member could get into one of the best cancer centers in the world, MD Anderson Cancer Center in Houston, Texas. He called the CEO of MD Anderson directly (when you're Ross Perot, everyone answers your call) and let him know that one of his employees was coming into the hospital. He then identified the lead physician who would be treating the employee and called him, too. He told the physician that he wanted daily updates on the progress being made to treat this individual's cancer and gave the doctor his personal cell phone number. He did this because he understood that if the team of physicians caring for his employee knew they would get a call from Ross Perot, a legendary businessman and a great patriot, his employee would get top priority.

It was in the presence of managers like Mr. Perot that I learned what a love-based business culture looks like. However, if you're still asking yourself what, besides running a successful healthcare consulting firm, gives me the right—the audacity—to tell you how and why to run a company imbued with a love-based culture, please know that I'm not relying on myself alone. Healthlink has spawned more CEOs who have started companies—more than 15 at last count—than any other company in the healthcare technology services industry. The leaders of these businesses experienced a love-based culture with us and are replicating it in their own companies. These are leaders who manage with teamwork, respect, and trust as their guiding lights.

I'm also not touting myself as a perfect example of a love-based leader. I was the CEO who pushed hard to get results with a strong focus on discipline. While I didn't think I was using fear as a motivator, people on the other end of my aggressive behavior might not have viewed it that way.

There are leaders who have worked for me who would not work for me again. There are even a few who would have described me at times as a bully, as someone who pushed too hard to move the company forward. I've often said that I felt like Star Trek's Captain Kirk yelling down to Scotty for more power, while Scotty is bouncing off the walls in the vibrating engine room, steam pouring out of every pipe, shouting back in his Scottish brogue: "I'm givin' her all she's got, Captain!"

OPERATING ON THE LOVE/FEAR CONTINUUM

As a leader, I didn't operate at full throttle in fear or love. Instead, I moved between the two within what I call the Love/Fear Continuum. I could invoke fear when I needed to move quickly because of an impending crisis. Likewise, I could be warm and motivating when appropriate. No one functions from a place of pure love or pure fear. We all operate within a range.

> A leader who never experiences fear is a leader who is being robbed of the opportunity to learn.

There are companies that lean toward fear-based leadership but show love on occasion, and there are love-based companies that need to make use of fear when a crisis requires "all hands on deck." A leader who never experiences fear is a leader who is being robbed of the opportunity to learn. It's through fear that we see the need for protection from forces that often are outside of our control. Fear is healthy when applied in the right context. (For more on this nuance, see chapter 7.)

I certainly felt this way as a leader. There were times when an employee needed compassion due to challenging problems at home or at work. In those cases, I extended Acts of Love without hesitation. That said, if there was a crisis, I sometimes felt the fire blowing out of my body, singeing anyone within a few hundred feet.

VOICE OF DANA

As an engineer, I'm happiest when a concept can be drawn out on a whiteboard in a tidy, clear way, or when a graph or spreadsheet captures exactly what we're talking about. When I think about a love-based culture, it's natural that a graph comes to mind:

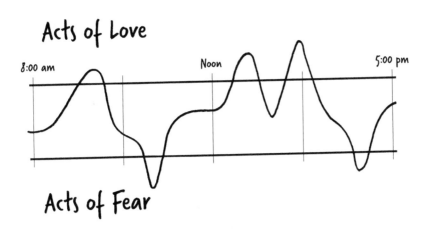

Having a love-based culture isn't defined by being in a love state all the time. Creating a love-based culture requires an ability to balance the sometimes-necessary state of fear with moments of true love.

Every leader and every company spends time in the fear zone, and we all spend time in the love zone, sometimes moving from one to the other in a heartbeat. Sometimes, it's business factors that dictate in what zone the leader will operate. Sometimes, it's an innate understanding of what people need that drives a leader into the love zone.

Ivo was a great leader because he knew how to move from one zone to the other when needed. If fear sounds like it's rarely needed, consider that fear of failure, when responded to strategically, can be a profound tool for motivation and growth. For much of our history at Healthlink, we were in hyper-growth mode. There was a tremendous demand for our services and we didn't want to disappoint anyone, so the whole company operated in fear mode much of the time. That is, we were afraid we couldn't meet demands, we were afraid we would make a mistake, and we were afraid we'd disappoint Ivo, our clients, or each other.

Ivo felt the pressures of the market demands and the opportunities they presented, and he responded by moving into fear mode. He'd set unreasonable deadlines, establishing goals that we felt we'd never meet. He pushed hard so that the company could meet its goals. None of us wanted to fail, especially not Ivo. I honestly don't believe we would have been the top-ranked services company in healthcare or been positioned for acquisition by IBM if he hadn't pushed us to be the best.

Operating in fear mode, even when necessary due to market pressures or corporate conditions, can be exhausting and can lead to burnout, but Ivo had an innate ability to balance the time he spent in fear mode by moving into love mode when people needed it. While the fear did create stress, the results of success made everyone feel like winners, much like sports teams who fight hard-fought battles and can bask in the light of victory after the game has ended.

There were times I'd feel exhausted, but as I'd reach the point where I felt I was out of steam, Ivo would move into love mode. He'd say what I needed to hear, or he'd surprise me with a personal, thoughtful gift. I'd walk away motivated, energized, and feeling love in the workplace.

In spite of the pressure Ivo brought to bear on the company, we had a tremendous amount of trust built into our culture. Health-link's employees knew they could do what was right for the client and felt empowered to make decisions without retribution if a decision had a bad result. Our company was wired for love and trust, and we only felt fear at times because of our intense desire to succeed.

Who wouldn't give 110% when fear of failure was balanced with such a strong sense of love and support? I'd frequently find out that Ivo had rewarded someone for behavior in accordance with our core values with a dinner out, a long weekend at a hotel with their significant other, or maybe flowers, just when they most needed a little love. He once even paid for me to have laser eye surgery to improve my vision. He told me that if he were to give me money, I'd spend it on my family, rather than on giving myself something special. I've enjoyed the gift of good vision now for 20 years. I'll never forget this Act of Love.

As Dana's comments suggest, we as humans rise to what-ever the occasion demands, with our emotions and survival instincts leading the way. Like I did, those who lead by love can and do experience fear, but they hopefully will arrive at a place of confidence that allows them to present their fears within their company and to customers in healthy, constructive ways, like tough love and encouraging pushes, not through scream-ing fights or a cycle of reactionary behavior.

During those times of pressure or of growth, the love/fear continuum's needle may peg hard to the fear side and operate in the red zone until the crisis is averted. What's important to understand is that in order to have a love-based culture, the needle needs to return to the love side of the continuum. Re-member, love is proactive; fear is reactive. If you err in one direction, be proactive and err toward love. When the needle errs toward the red zone of fear, chronic fear sets in and can cause long-term damage.

> Remember, love is proactive; fear is reactive. If you err in one direction, be proactive and err toward love.

What were the triggers that snapped me in and out of fear and love? Clearly, my trigger for moving into fear-based man-agement was driven by my fear of failure, one with which any entrepreneurial and C-suite readers may be familiar. There would be an impending deal on the horizon that I knew we could win, but I would still get this bad feeling in my gut that we weren't putting our best foot forward. That feeling would gnaw at me all day and all night until *bam!* Arms and legs would start moving, questions would be asked, directives would go out, and EVERYONE and EVERYTHING would get focused on WINNING.

Sometimes that fear-motivated behavior made the difference between winning and losing, and other times I was just flat-out irritating to a bunch of people who were doing their best to methodically prepare a presentation. When I would

Love-Based Culture Continuum

Fear-Based Culture Continuum

come out of my fear-of-failure fog and see the results of everyone kicking into high gear, all driving towards the same common goal, I'd dial it back toward love.

Even love-based companies need leaders to turn up the heat from time to time. Most businesses live in industries where competition is fierce, so being on your game means everything. This is similar to the environment our caveman ancestors experienced, who needed fear to avoid danger. Today, we have the same instincts. Our ancestors didn't experience fear all the time, though. Chronic fear was unlikely in their vocabularies, but it is an unfortunate habit in ours. Moving back to love, once the crisis, opportunity, or danger has been addressed, is key to a love-based culture and requires leaders who understand how important it is to take a deep breath, relax, and return to love.

THE COSTS OF LOVE AND FEAR

As you read this book, understand that building a love-based culture can be expensive. It costs time, patience, and money. When you demonstrate love, you focus on customer service and on making your employees, customers, and team happy. You want to deliver more than is expected.

At Healthlink, we focused on a culture of 100% referenceability—that is, 100% of our customers would and could serve as positive referral sources for us—to ensure that the entire team was laser-focused on dynamic customer service. As you will see, this is a theme that runs throughout this book. Setting a 100% goal is the first principle of a love-based culture and the one from which the other nine originate.

Our goal of 100% referenceability required us to cover related costs in hopes of getting a big return on our investment.

Love-based costs for Healthlink included:

» Additional training of employees so they clearly understood the products, methods, processes, and culture of our company

» The cost of hiring people who managed a quality process in order to let us learn about problems early enough to fix them before they became monumental

» Costs tied to processes and people's time for regular meetings and communication

» Costs related to developing replicable processes so that projects performed on the West Coast were executed the same way on the East Coast, thus reducing variation and error

» Costs tied to rigorous recruiting that ensured that the people we hired could deliver on our goal of 100% referenceability

Sometimes, in a love-based culture, there is also the cost of reduced revenue: you may have to refund money to customers who don't believe you've delivered on the promise that you sold them.

At a company that is hyper-focused on its customers, though, more projects work properly the first time because less energy is needed to resolve conflicts. Far less money is spent on supporting sales teams because of the trust that's been developed between your company and your existing customers. The high quality of your employees' work will lead to more assignments. Best of all, your customers will become your unpaid sales force, recommending you to their colleagues because of their satisfaction with your services. As a result, the cost of sales becomes lower because you can provide more services to existing happy customers.

Fear-based competitors aren't going to have the costs I mentioned above. This could make them more profitable or allow them to undercut your price in a pitch war. But fear-based companies have their own hidden costs.

In a fear-based culture:

» Leaders manage through subtle manipulation, dominance, and an "I'm smarter than you" attitude.

» Employees hesitate to speak up and often try to hide their errors. When a problem is detected later, it will have grown and become more difficult to correct.

» Everyone is out for themselves. This may lead to employees withholding valuable information from colleagues.

» Value statements hang on the walls of conference rooms, yet nobody cares about them because management doesn't practice what they preach.

» People pass the buck so as not to be the person who gets blamed for an unpopular decision. Customer responses are therefore delayed.

» Titles are an important indicator of success.

» Decisions are based on a zero-sum principle. For me to win, you must lose.

» Executives believe that money is the primary motivator for people. Management systems only focus on individual performance measures and bank on those measures to determine compensation.

» Being summoned to the boss's office invokes terror and causes people to think about who they can blame for anything they might be accused of.

» There is a sense of "one strike and you're out." This inhibits productive risk-taking and innovation.

» Everyone becomes a clock-watcher.

» The company is slow to identify people who don't fit into the culture or who can't perform in their jobs.

» The company risks alienating one of its most significant resources: its team.

» Employees commonly report that they feel like they can't afford to take a sick day, and won't ask for time off to attend a child's performance or to take a sick parent to the doctor because it might reflect poorly on them in their performance review. They miss out on critical life events and resent the company.

» People feel tension and insecurity in an atmosphere of secrecy and mistrust.

» The goal is "me" above all else.

PERFORM ACTS OF LOVE TO COMBAT FEAR

If you're reading this and you're currently on the job hunt, beware of fear-based businesses that pretend to have a love-based culture. For instance, many workers now constantly check their email to show their bosses how available they are. This would be fine if it were considered above and beyond the call of duty, but more often than not, being chained to one's phone is the expected norm. More striking is the fact that some companies have doctors' offices, gyms, dormitories, and other amenities on their corporate campuses, increasingly insuring that their workers hardly ever have to leave. This may look like love, in that the companies are providing resources to their employees, but in the end, this behavior may be motivated by a chronic fear for their bottom line, not a concern for the health of their human workers.

For those of you who work at companies with fear-based cultures, this book may help you learn how to change your corporate culture or, if change is not possible, show you what to look for in your next job. Many of you have given up hope that your company could ever have a higher calling, much less show compassion in the workplace. If that is the case, I urge you to read the Acts of Love that are sprinkled throughout this book. These are real letters from people who have experienced unique examples of kindness in the workplace that showed that somebody cared about them.

I received these letters in response to a simple request I posted on Facebook and LinkedIn: "Has a boss, a vendor, or a peer done something for you at work that showed that they cared? Attended your dad's funeral? Sent you on a trip? Gone the extra mile to help you with a project? I'm looking for examples of kind acts done at work that blew you away." I received hundreds of responses, some going back more than 30 years. What you'll find is that everyone can make their mark simply by showing a little kindness each day that they go to work.

Of all the responses I received, how many do you believe involved money? A raise, an unexpected bonus, or perhaps some stock options? The answer?

ZERO, ZIP, NADA. *Not a single memory of an Act of Love involved compensation.*

Most of the letters came from people who were grateful that their boss had attended a family member's funeral, given them time off to care for a family member, or simply shown appreciation for their efforts.

As you read these Acts of Love, think about how you could make a difference in someone's life. Think about it everyday. If necessary, change your routine so that committing Acts of Love becomes the norm rather than the exception. Regardless of whether you have any control over your company's billion-dollar culture, commit Acts of Love and you will change that culture, one small act at a time.

INTRODUCING THE 10 PRINCIPLES OF A LOVE-BASED CULTURE

What is key to creating a love-based culture is that every employee embraces the culture and owns it. Policies, procedures, and processes all have to be aligned. When bad things happened and tough decisions needed to be made at Healthlink, we had to stay true to our values and avoid the temptation to revert to old behaviors.

Though I had a vision for the principles of a love-based culture as I began writing this book, they were based more on a feeling than on any objective data. However, by the time I had written the last chapter, I realized that a list had emerged, much to the delight of my more detail-oriented, compulsive, and list-worshiping editors, co-writers, and reviewers.

While I wish business were so simple that I could publish the five things you can do today to create a love-based business, it isn't. Every company is different, and how your leadership, compensation programs, HR policies, quality standards, and other processes can support a healthy culture will vary. However, I do believe that the 10 principles, which you will see explained below and explored in detail in the coming chapters, are common threads that relate to most businesses. The questions associated with each principle at the ends of the chapters can act as a guide or scorecard for your company.

So, if you want to know if you have a love-based culture, see how many of the following 10 statements you can honestly apply to your company. Not all of these principles need to be true in order to create a love-based culture, but if your company has too many fear-based elements, this list can help you identify how to move your needle toward love.

100% Referenceability

Become obsessed with a bold, customer-centered goal.

My company has a goal of 100% customer satisfaction. We would have no business without clients who believe in my company because of our outstanding products and services.

Leadership

Put your employees' needs ahead of your own.

The executives at my company put their employees' needs above their own. I trust the leadership of my company. They care about me.

Core Values

Be uncompromising in living core values daily.

I know, understand, and feel ownership of my company's core values. The executives at my company "walk the talk." I feel safe working for my company.

A Higher Calling

Have purpose beyond profits.

I believe my company is passionate about how we contribute to the greater good of society. I can pursue a higher calling by working at my company.

Governance

Focus on long-term growth.

My company's board of directors holds executives accountable for the long-term success of the company, not only for meeting short-term financial goals. The directors are not at risk of being surprised due to a lack of transparency in my company.

Compensation
Reward those who add value.
My compensation is based on my company's success and on the overall value I provide in contributing to that success. It is not solely metrics-driven. I trust my manager to pay me fairly. My company rewards an employee's value to the company regardless of their success in achieving their individual performance goals.

Winning
Feel the buzz of success.
My company makes me feel like a winner because of the overwhelming positive energy I feel every day when I come to work. I work hard because I want to make my company successful.

The 3 Ps: Policies, Processes, Performance
Hardwire processes to trust.
The policies in my company are based on trust rather than on penalties. The processes in my company support teamwork. My manager and I have productive, two-way, honest, and candid conversations about my performance.

Decision-Making
Empower those closest to the customer to do what's right.
The managers of my company are empowered to make decisions (within predetermined boundaries) that impact customers. I feel trusted to show good judgment to solve problems without asking for permission.

Acts of Love
Show that you care.
The executives of my company perform acts of love for their team. As an employee, I have benefited from acts of kindness.

LOVE IS A CHOICE

One last thought as you move into the heart of this book. If you want to build a love-based culture, you'll need to unlearn much of what you've been taught in the past about the roles of HR processes, compensation programs, performance metrics, organizational charts, leadership, office layouts, and other policies.

Rethink EVERYTHING.

If you walk into your office with an air of superiority because you are the CEO, then you're missing a key point. You are the CEO because that's the role for which you are uniquely qualified and at which you excel. You are not better or higher or superior in any way to anybody else in the company. You have simply been blessed with skills that allow you to build a business, serve, and lead others to achieve their best in their roles, and to help them grow whenever possible.

> Regardless of whether you have any control over your company's billion-dollar culture, commit Acts of Love and you will change that culture, one small act at a time.

I've seen what happens when a company's culture is stronger than I am as its leader. I've experienced what it feels like when a love-based culture challenges me to make decisions that are in the long-term best interests of the company rather than decisions that simply reduce short-term pain. The power of brotherly and sisterly love in the workplace fuels growth by people who truly care.

Who wouldn't want to work for a company where they are trusted to not only make decisions, but also to make mistakes, with an understanding that everything is a learning process and that these mistakes will help take the company to the next level? Learning from mistakes is part of the human growth process. How you respond to them reflects your company's love- or fear-based culture.

Who wouldn't want to lead a company where, as they walk the halls of the office, they see the smiling faces of people who aren't afraid to look them in the eye? Where people work hard, share ideas, and put in extra effort because they want to be there, not because they have to be there?

Who wouldn't want to invest in a company where they know that every employee understands that their role is to add value, regardless of what their individual performance goals say?

And what customer wouldn't want to do business with a company when they know that every team member absolutely owns the goal of making them a happy, referenceable client?

My goal is to create believers in the reality that a business can have a love-based culture and grow with higher profits than its fear-based competitors.

So, let's get busy; we've got a lot of love to do.

1

100% REFERENCEABILITY:
Become Obsessed with a Bold, Customer-Centered Goal

It shouldn't come as a surprise that the first principle of a love-based culture focuses on giving customers the best-quality product or service. When this is the case, quality should, as the old saying goes, start at the top. What the "top" can do is set the bar high and then assume the responsibility of providing the kind of leadership needed for every employee of every rank to achieve the goal.

But not all quality goals are equal. Take this one, set by Håkan Samuelsson, the president and CEO of Volvo Cars Corporation: "Our vision is that by 2020 no one should be killed or seriously injured in a new Volvo car."[1]

The downstream ramifications of that statement are enormous. Samuelsson didn't say, "By 2020 almost no one should be safe from death or injury." He didn't say "fewer than 10% of all drivers and pedestrians." He said *no one*, and in doing so, he set an all-or-nothing quality goal. All processes, policies, procedures, and yes, the Volvo culture need to be aligned to achieve it. It takes far more than just a bold statement from the CEO to make a goal like this a reality.

SETTING THE HIGHEST POSSIBLE GOAL FOR CUSTOMER SERVICE

I learned this lesson the hard way in the early days of Health-link. We held a board meeting at which our chairman, Rod Canion (founder and CEO of Compaq Computers), stated that he didn't see any reason why we should set a goal that allowed even one customer to be unhappy. I couldn't rationalize any way that he was wrong. Because we didn't have any metrics for happiness, we decided that our quality metric would be that every one of our customers would be referenceable.

PRINCIPLE #1

100% REFERENCEABILITY
Become Obsessed with a Bold, Customer-Centered Goal

Love-based cultures set quality goals high, with the customer at the center of the circle. What's more, setting the goal that every client will act as a positive reference for you to their peers demonstrates the importance of customers to your team.

We defined Healthlink's goal of 100% referenceability simply as the positive recommendation that our key client contacts would give to others who were seeking partners to hire for their projects. Since we provided services for healthcare systems doing IT strategy and implementation services, most of our key contacts tended to be chief information officers (CIOs). We were lucky to be operating in the healthcare technology industry, where CIOs have a strong network of peers. While there was a formal reference process to be completed for all major project procurements, CIOs also made personal phone calls to their closest peers to get the "real story" on a potential vendor. Often, these were multimillion-dollar, highly visible projects that, if improperly executed, would result in CIOs losing their jobs, receivables skyrocketing, and patient care being impacted. No executive in the healthcare organization was going to give a reference that was undeserving, considering the stakes involved.

Of course, setting a goal is the easy part. Doing it, on the other hand, is not so easy. Our quality metric was put to the test a week after it was invented. Following the board meeting at which we set the bar at 100% client referenceability, we went on a management retreat to take goals like this one to the next level. I was still basking in the glow of that retreat on a calm Friday afternoon, but as I was packing up to head out for a weekend with my family, the phone rang. On the other end was Chuck, a long-time client.

"Ivo, we have a problem."

My ears perked up at those words. I set my bag down and said, "So, what's up, Chuck?" He proceeded to describe a project that was strategic to his success that had found itself in the ditch. He had an executive presentation coming up with all of his peers and bosses in a few weeks and did not feel like the quality of the work Healthlink had done was good enough to share. He wanted us out, and somebody else in.

Without hesitation, I said, "Chuck, I know you're probably slammed next week, but I'm going to fly to Newark on Monday and be in your office by 7:30 a.m. Don't worry about getting to me on Monday morning or even that day. I won't have a return flight set up, so whenever you can meet with me is fine. Good-bye."

I hung up the phone and let out a deep sigh as I looked down at my notes from our retreat. Guess what was staring me right in my face?

100%

100% - in big, black, bold print.

When Chuck came in on Monday morning, I was sitting outside his office. He stopped, took a few seconds to stare at me, then, without saying a word, raised his hand and beckoned to me with his finger. I got up and followed him into his office. I spent all morning with him, using a whiteboard to understand the problem, and I didn't end up leaving until Thursday of that week. Because Chuck thought it would be helpful, I came back and personally gave the presentation to his executive team to a standing ovation. As I left the office, I shook Chuck's hand. The only image in my mind was this: 100%.

Done.

Little did I know that my actions were reverberating throughout the company, from the East Coast to the West. I had always heard that "quality starts at the top," and as is the case with most executives, I had paid lip service to this phrase without really understanding what it meant. None of our employees wanted to be on the project where Ivo had to fly in to meet with their client. This was partially because I was the CEO, and however hard I tried to make everyone at Health-link feel at home with me, some still held onto their baggage from previous employers. Secondly, I really sucked as a consultant. For me to personally come in and "save" a project was a big stretch. I did, however, have great relationship skills that could create some cover while the real consultants worked their magic.

While there was a factor of fear among our employees never wanting to be the first to fail, far more overwhelming was a sense of pride that allowed our people to be part of a company where they could put their reputation on the line and know everybody, from their teammates to the CEO, had their back.

I felt 100% referenceability weighing heavily on my shoulders as I flew home to Houston that week. This goal would become the single biggest driving force in Healthlink's processes, culture, and leadership style. This single most important goal spoke to our ability to acquire clients and hire the best people in the industry. It created a filter for hiring senior management that asked, "Is this person too fancy and dated to roll up their sleeves and fix real problems for our clients?"

100% IS IMPOSSIBLE IN A CULTURE OF FEAR

In the end, 100% referenceability helped make Healthlink the fastest-growing and highest-quality consulting firm in our industry. Year after year we were considered one of the best companies to work for in all of healthcare. After 13 years, having provided services to hundreds of clients, performed thousands of projects, and billed hundreds of millions of dollars, we were still able to proudly proclaim 100% customer satisfaction.

This quality metric as a goal became all-consuming for the simple reason that achieving it resulted in a company that everyone in the industry wanted to work for; where we won, won, won and rarely lost deals; where we were ranked No. 1 in KLAS, the *Consumer Reports* of healthcare, year after year; and where investors were able to enjoy the ever-increasing value of their investments with no risk of liabilities or surprises. Sound like a fantasy? It's not. In our 13 years as a 100%-referenceable company, we never had a dollar of bad debt, never defended ourselves against a formal lawsuit, and in all but one year, we achieved our financial targets.

This could never have been accomplished without a love-based culture in which teamwork was paramount and all employees, from the receptionist to the C-suite to the salespeople and consultants in the field, totally owned our commitment to customer satisfaction.

Neither Dana nor I purposely set out to create a love-based culture; it emerged from a team of people who respected and trusted each other, valued teamwork, and felt empowered to make decisions. Our HR policies, compensation programs, and core processes were all designed to accommodate a culture that put our customers first and respected our employees' desire to be associated with a high-quality enterprise.

When the prime objective is to have 100%-referenceable customers, a love-based culture must exist. If it doesn't, employees won't feel comfortable asking for help; putting their problem projects into red status; or admitting they made a mistake with an understanding that, the sooner we jump on it, the more likely it is we can fix the problem. Fear-based cultures penalize employees for making mistakes, intimidate subordinates, and have processes in place that puts punishment over the value of learning lessons.

The intensity, commitment, and dedication required to be a 100%-referenceable company require a workforce of people who are driven by aspirations that go well beyond those of a typical job. Employees want meaning in their life beyond a day-to-day grind. They want to connect and contribute to something beyond themselves. These are the people who will go the extra mile and thrive in a love-based culture. In our case, they were healthcare professionals who had a strong desire to improve the health of large populations by delivering solutions to healthcare providers. Letting even one of those providers down would have been a slap in the face to our company's higher calling. The company culture, which connected, respected, and loved its employees, supported their commitment to each other and to the success of the company.

> The intensity, commitment, and dedication required to be a 100%-referenceable company require a workforce of people who are driven by aspirations that go well beyond those of a typical job.

KEY ELEMENTS TO ACHIEVING YOUR CUSTOMER-FACING GOALS

To be a 100%-referenceable company, we realized we needed processes and tools to be part of the solutions we sold. That way, variation would be minimized between projects and any lessons learned would be applied to future projects through our training programs.

Whether your customer-facing goal is to be 100% referenceable, to have no one die from car safety issues, or to put an astronaut on Mars, it will require two key elements to be achieved: (1) a foundation in a quality methodology and (2) a customer-facing culture of open communication.

A FOUNDATION IN QUALITY METHODOLOGY

First, I recommend pursuing highly disciplined compliance to any one of a number of great quality programs. For instance, you might check out Kaizen, Zero Defects Programs, Six Sigma, Quality Circle, Taguchi Methods, the Toyota Production System, Kansei Engineering, TRIZ, BPR, OQRM, ISO, or Top-Down & Bottom-Up.

All of these programs have common denominators: They all want to reduce variation. They all require leadership, teamwork, and communication. In fact, all of these quality programs pay a great deal of attention to the importance of corporate culture. Their methodologies use teams to find and address issues and therefore need an environment of open communication to solve problems.

Once you've selected a quality program to follow, you must ask yourself if you are implementing a quality process or implementing a new culture that will enable these new processes to succeed. Changing processes is the commodity component of quality, but the stickiness of the change has everything to do with culture. While on the surface it may appear that a process has changed, the changes won't work in the long term without a culture that embraces the change. Otherwise, old processes will snap back into place like a rubber band. Culture is what allows process change to become integrated into the character of a business. The higher the bar, the more important culture becomes.

Again, let me be clear. Adopting a quality program is not about checking items off of a list. Too often, managers want to do nothing more than to check the box on clearly outlined tasks that accompany adherence to a quality program. Define the problems? Check! Define the customer requirements?

Check! Document current processes? Check! Gather baseline data? Check! Brainstorm solutions? Check! Check! Check! Check! Check! Done.

> Changing processes is the commodity component of quality, but the stickiness of the change has everything to do with culture.

But it's not done. Comprehensive, enterprise-wide change involves employee alignment to a common goal. Checking the boxes works well for those who believe that leadership is more about structure than people. Granted, structure is important, but the long-term impact of checking off all those boxes requires more than a spreadsheet. It requires more than being highly disciplined in executing each step of the methodology. It requires a culture that embraces the ultimate goal of the program, which is made up of the people who own it and contribute to it.

Shifting the culture of a company to one that can implement a great quality program takes not only an outstanding quality methodology, it also requires great leadership, starting with investors and directors, compensation programs, and policies that support teamwork, as well as a management system that is built on trusting those who are close to clients to make decisions. This ties together when all eyes are on the customer.

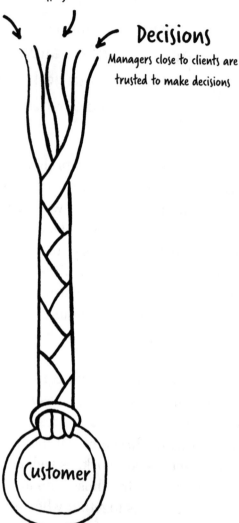

Processes
HR and financial controls protect the company without handcuffing those who run it.

Leadership
Investors, board of directors, and executive teams are aligned on core values, are transparent, and manage with trust.

Decisions
Managers close to clients are trusted to make decisions

Customer

More than Leadership
It all has to tie together

VOICE OF DANA

Our employees always set the example for me when it came to putting the customer first. I could tell story after story of how our employees went the extra mile and put customer needs above all else. One that really made an impression on me had to do with a small county hospital that was going through tough financial times even as they implemented a new electronic health record. They needed a lot of help, but they really couldn't afford much. We contracted with them to provide one Healthlink employee to train their staff on the new system. Because money was so tight, we agreed to a fixed number of hours at a fixed fee. The organization successfully implemented their system, and I thought we were done.

A year later, out of the blue, a check showed up for some additional hours of work. I thought it was a mistake, and I called the customer. He told me that as they had approached their "live" date, they were incredibly shorthanded. Our employee knew that she had only been contracted to work a specific number of hours but had decided on her own that she would make sure that the customer was successful. Without seeking permission, she had worked extra hours. Lots of extra hours—nights and weekends—leading up to the deadline.

The customer told me that he couldn't afford to pay us then, but he never forgot how she had put his hospital's success first. He said that things had improved financially, and the purchase order was to pay us for the extra time that she had put in.

If that purchase order hadn't shown up, I might never have known how our employee had put the customer first.

A CUSTOMER-FACING CULTURE OF OPEN COMMUNICATION

In addition to whatever quality methodology you've chosen to implement, make sure the following cultural components of early detection and fast response are addressed.

They focus on transparency; trust; and quick, direct communication both internally and externally at all levels of the organizational chart. Identifying problems quickly, escalating them appropriately, and learning from them didn't happen at Healthlink just because we encouraged it. It happened because we built a business infrastructure with policies and procedures that supported identifying problems early enough that they could be tackled without blame. These processes included:

A Peer-Based Quality Review Process - A peer, not a manager, reviewed every project monthly. This process encouraged open, non-recriminatory dialogue and prompt discussion of potential problems.

An Escalation Process - Anyone in the company could declare a project "yellow" or "red" depending on the severity of the problem at hand. Clearly defined mechanisms would kick into place to engage senior management and appropriate subject-matter experts so that the problem could be resolved quickly. No one was ever blamed for declaring a red or yellow status; we encouraged people to step forward as soon as they became aware of a problem. Our philosophy was that escalation was simply a way of saying, "I need help."

Call to Action - When someone had an urgent issue, they could declare the need for a "Call to Action." This was a particular escalation process that was used when a problem needed the immediate attention of senior leadership. When a Call to Action was initiated, everyone dropped what they were doing and focused on solving the problem.

Lessons Learned - After a problem occurred, we'd conduct formal "Lessons Learned" sessions. These were non-judgmental sessions in which we asked, "What did we do right? What could we have done better, and what do we need to change so that this problem doesn't happen again?" Frequently, the outcome of a Lessons Learned session was a change in methodology or process so that we could make sure we didn't repeat the actions that had caused the problem in the first place.

When our people realized that they could participate in these sessions without incurring any negative consequences, there was open discussion, which contributed to a constant learning environment. Everyone was encouraged to speak up early in the process. This helped us act efficiently to serve our customers as well and as quickly as possible.

BRINGING IT TOGETHER

What is key to creating a love-based culture is that every employee embraces the culture and owns it. At Healthlink, our policies, procedures, and processes all had to be aligned. When bad things happened and tough decisions needed to be made, we had to stay true to our values and not revert to old, fear-based behaviors.

Love-based cultures require an all-in attitude in which every aspect of the business incorporates the concepts of teamwork, trust, and love. For example, changing your communications strategy without changing compensation or decision-making strategies will not result in a love-based culture. Establishing goals that are not supported by the policies of the HR department or the metrics and management processes of the CFO could quickly result in the core values posted on the wall of the conference room being laughed at by your employees. In short, if it all doesn't tie together, it's not a love-based culture. It's a sham.

> **Love-based cultures require an all-in attitude in which every aspect of the business incorporates the concepts of teamwork, trust, and love.**

These practices were reinforced in Healthlink employee culture by the way that meetings opened with a brief discussion of core values and ended with what we called "Bs & Cs," Benefits and Concerns. I loved the way Dana would open the Bs & Cs discussion with this speech:

"Let's take a few minutes at the end of this meeting to capture what's on our minds that is good or of concern. No one will argue with your ideas. They are your perceptions only and therefore are valid. Let's start with benefits. What's on your mind that is a benefit of this meeting or of our project as a whole?" The facilitator would capture ideas as verbatim as possible, moving quickly. After several ideas had been captured, the facilitator would say: "Now let's turn to concerns. What's on your mind that is of concern about this meeting or our project as a whole?"

We took special care that no individual comment was judged or minimized in these sessions. This was a safe place for employees to discuss tangible and intangible concerns. Often a concern would be voiced during Bs & Cs that hadn't come up in the meeting but that was critical to the project. For example, there may have been no place on the agenda for someone's feeling that the team was burned out and prone to error or that an important client hadn't participated in key meetings. Anything and everything was game for discussion during Bs & Cs, and we found that they frequently made a big difference in keeping projects from jumping into red status. What was once one person's concern, which may have been swallowed and taken back to the cubicles as gossip fodder in a fear-based company, now became everyone's concern.

The practice of opening meetings with a discussion of our core values set a tone in the company that these principles were to be respected by everyone. Ending every meeting with Bs & Cs validated a culture where open discussion was encouraged. These practices were taught in our orientation classes and reinforced by leadership day after day, month after month, and year after year. They reduced fear of repercussions for mistakes and turned them into teaching moments instead. Guilt was replaced with the pride our people felt in knowing that they were putting their best foot forward as a team. It's practices like these that create a love-based culture.

VOICE OF DANA

I remember that in one Benefits & Concerns session a concern caused us to make a major change to a project. We had been working for several weeks on analysis, the first step in helping an academic medical center choose a new electronic health record. To us, the answer was pretty obvious. There was one solution that could be implemented in a fraction of the time, at a fraction of the cost, and that would deliver a solid, working process.

I mean, really, who wouldn't want the least expensive, fastest solution with proven results?

We presented our recommendation to the health system's executive team and lead physicians. We were met with positive feedback from administrators and especially from the finance folks, who liked the fact that we were recommending the least expensive solution. Feeling pretty good, we decided to wrap up with benefits and concerns.

The minute we got to concerns, a physician who had been quiet throughout the meeting stood up. His face turned red as he spoke out passionately, "Where's the physician perspective in this recommendation? I see how this makes the most sense from a timeline and cost perspective, but what about MY perspective? Who cares if I just don't want to use the system that is fastest or least expensive? How will it do anyone any good to implement a solution the physicians WON'T USE?"

I suspect this physician was somewhat reluctant to voice his angst in front of his peers and all the health system executives, but the non-confrontational way we approached benefits and concerns gave him a setting where he felt comfortable bringing his issue forward. Once he spoke, the dam broke. Other physicians voiced their concerns, too.

By the time we left the meeting, it was clear we had to go back to the drawing board. Fast and cheap really didn't matter if the key users wanted a different solution. If we hadn't done our Benefits & Concerns exercise, we might have traveled far down the road before we realized we had to make a course correction.

WHY 99% ISN'T ENOUGH

In light of the lessons shared in this chapter, take some time to read the goals that are set by most companies. You'll find words like "be the premiere _____," "superior market execution," "sustainable growth," or "lead the way." Though they make us feel good, most of these words don't force an executive team to rethink the kind of culture they need to operate at the highest possible level of quality. Setting the bar high requires a workforce that buys into a goal and is dedicated to making it happen. It's their goal, too, not just the CEO's.

Over the course of my career, I've found the gap between 99% and 100% to be bigger than the gap between 1% and 99%. Most companies won't set the bar at the highest possible level because they fear that last 1%, the totally unreasonable customer that nobody can make happy. But if you lower expectations by 1%, why not 2%? Or 5%? I mean, why not? Maybe Volvo should set a goal that only 10 people will die in a new Volvo car in 2022.

> Over the course of my career, I've found the gap between 99% and 100% to be bigger than the gap between 1% and 99%.

An added bonus: I doubt Volvo's competitors are sitting around a conference table, rationalizing how they've ensured their success by setting the bar low. Instead, they're waking up and taking notice of Volvo's all-or-nothing safety goal. If I'm an executive at a competing auto manufacturer, I'm wondering if I need to raise the bar, too.

Be bold. Shoot for the moon.

PRINCIPLE #1

100% REFERENCEABILITY
Become Obsessed with a Bold, Customer-Centered Goal

When it comes to your company's goals, be uncompromising. Be bold. Build your goals with an all-or-nothing attitude of love. Incorporate your 100% standard into all of your processes, policies, and procedures; your core values; and your customer-facing interactions. Then watch as you reap the benefits.

Call to Action:

» What is a high standard or quality metric that can become your company's version of "100%"?

» Are your company's goals owned by those who must achieve them? Or are there only negative consequences for failing to meet the goals?

» Are you trusted to make decisions that are responsive to your customer's problems and needs? Or do you have to go through deep layers of approval before you can help them out?

» Do you feel comfortable asking for help at work? Or do you fear that you'll be disciplined for exposing a problem?

My Lessons Learned:

» Much stronger synergies were created from Dana's and my vastly different management styles than if we had shared personality traits. One plus one equals ten when opposites balance each other out, while working toward a common set of values.

» A love-based company's costs of additional training, communications, quality processes, and recruiting pale in comparison to the costs of fear-based companies who lose unhappy clients, get sued, and have bad debt. A love-based culture enables higher profits in the long run.

» If you are the CEO, you will know that you have a good culture when it controls you, rather than you controlling the culture you helped build. You don't own it; your employees do. When a love-based company's CEO doesn't respect its culture and the culture kicks their ass, then the culture is working extremely well.

» The gap between 99% and 100% referenceable is a bigger gap than the one between 1% and 99%. Being able to solve for the 1% of customers that anyone else would give up on creates the magic that makes your company special.

ACTS OF LOVE

When I became a mother, I wanted to continue my work, including finishing projects that had been building for years. To accomplish these goals required traveling within a month or two of giving birth, but I also wanted to spend that precious time with my baby and breastfeed him. I struggled when I was away from my child for more than a day or two.

When she learned about my dilemma, my boss did something extraordinary. She paid for a nanny to fly with me on my business trips and stay in a separate hotel room so that my baby could come with me. The nanny dropped me off at my meetings, and then explored the city with the baby. They would come back to my meetings when my son was hungry, and I was able to call a break every four to six hours to feed him.

As a result, my son was with me every night for most of his first year. That allowed me to further my career, meet my customer commitments, and give my son a great start. Fifteen months later, my boss did it again when I had my second son. She always maintained that it was worth it. She created no sense of guilt and made no comments about my special treatment, much less any "you owe me" baggage. That gesture meant so much to my family and me.

2

LEADERSHIP:
Put Your Employees' Needs Ahead of Your Own

Around the time I was peaking in business, my parents lived next door to me. I remember going over to their house whenever I was back in town. I would sit in the same chair, right across from them, in their tiny living room.

Once, my mom asked me, "So, how many people work for you?" At the time my response was around 600. I'll never forget what she said next: "That's a lot of families to be responsible for."

Just like that, in my mind, billable units quickly turned into souls with children. Moms tend to cut to the chase, and sometimes straight to the heart of the matter. I never forgot her words.

According to the second principle, a love-based culture is only as strong as its leadership is authentic.

Let's be honest, none of us has walked on water or been anointed a guru. It's unlikely that any of us are currently self-actualized and at the peak of Abraham Maslow's Hierarchy of Needs. We all enjoy recognition and the encouragement that goes along with it, but if our own rewards come at the expense of the teams we lead, then we are fear-based leaders.

PRINCIPLE #2

LEADERSHIP
Put Your Employees' Needs Ahead of Your Own

Love-based leaders put their teams first. They do this because it is the best way to add overall value to the company.

I'm not the only one who thinks so. Alan Mulally is a remarkable leader who puts love high on his list of priorities. The former president and CEO of the Ford Motor Company turned his business around when it was on the verge of failure. He didn't do this by being a fear-based leader. He did it by operating under the credo: "The purpose of life is to love and be loved."[1]

Third-richest man in the world Warren Buffet's definition of success can also be summed up in one word: love. He suggests incorporating success into your business life by "choos[ing] a culture of love," his way of describing an environment in which people love coming to work.[2]

What's more, as CEO of Healthlink, I had the opportunity to work with Rod Canion and two other former Compaq executives. They were all investors in Healthlink and members of my board of directors. Rod built Compaq Computers from nothing into a multibillion-dollar company. His greatest influence on Healthlink was setting the quality metric of having 100% referenceability, which we covered in chapter 1.

Compaq is a great example of a love-based global company. As a fellow Texan, I watched Rod build it into not only the fastest-growing company in business at the time, but also into a company whose products were of the highest quality in their industry. Everyone wanted to work at Compaq. It was known for being an employee-friendly company that was clearly the place to work in Houston.

Earlier, I mentioned Ross Perot. Mort Meyerson was the man responsible for building Ross' companies and making him billions of dollars at Electronic Data Systems. EDS was also a love-based company due, in part, to Ross and Mort hiring a large number of ex-military managers. While the U.S. military may have a reputation for being highly disciplined and dealing efficiently with crisis situations, it also takes care of its people and depends on loyalty.

Mort was the visionary, the big thinker, with a maniacal attention to detail. He has been a co-investor in several of my companies. While most investors focus primarily on a company's financial picture, Mort probes much deeper. I connect with Mort because he leads with intuition. Résumés are meaningless to him. He interviews for character, integrity, and grit. He looks for winners, regardless of a person's pedigree.

WHAT IS LOVE-BASED LEADERSHIP?

For me, love-based leadership is bound up in authenticity, in showing your team who you are and who they should be following. It's easier for an employee to do this when the person they're following feels "real." To be an authentic leader, you must lead with self-awareness, vulnerability, transparency, and forgiveness.

Leading With Self-Awareness

While most leaders want to operate at a high level of consciousness, believing in unconditional love and a diminishment of their selfish egos, they also need to be self-aware when it comes to their feelings and character. One of the worst things you can do as a leader is to present yourself as selfless when, in fact, you are not.

10 – 15% of people are SELF AWARE

85 – 90% of people are OBLIVIOUS to how they are viewed by others

In 2014, organizational psychologist Tasha Eurich conducted a large-scale scientific study of self-awareness. In 10 separate investigations featuring nearly 5,000 participants, her team found that only 10 to 15% of those surveyed qualified as "self-aware," that is, having the ability to see themselves clearly.[3]

The study defines two categories of self-awareness. The first, *internal self-awareness*, reflects how clearly we view our values, goals, feelings, strengths, weaknesses, and our impact on other people. The second category, *external self-awareness*, refers to understanding how other people view us.

I can easily see how fear-based managers would lack self-awareness. Who would ever want to admit that they manage with fear? On the other hand, I suspect that many business leaders think they operate in a love-based culture when they do not. All leaders need trusted peers who will provide them with honest feedback. Moreover, they need to be open with those peers so they can become truly self-aware. Yes, this means making themselves vulnerable. If they aren't open to receiving honest criticism or feel uncomfortable about facing it, that indicates a need for introspection.

Being self-aware doesn't, by itself, make you a compassionate, authentic, and selfless leader. It will, however, give you a baseline for evaluating your strengths and weaknesses, and may provide the opportunity for you to become a leader who can create a love-based culture. After all, how can you improve if you don't even know who you are? The best way to know if your perception of yourself is accurate is by gathering information from people all around you: your superiors, subordinates, peers, and customers. This is why 360-degree feedback programs are helpful in enhancing self-awareness. (See the first section under "How to Become a Love-Based Leader" on page 35 for more information.)

Leading With Vulnerability

People who build love-based cultures don't view vulnerability as a weakness. Instead, they see it as exhibiting the courage to be authentic and to allow their employees a peek behind the veil. It involves caring deeply even at the risk of feeling pain and disappointment. It requires recognizing one's flaws and even being able to laugh at them. It means failing and being willing to admit it. Being vulnerable is the essence of being human. Most people will voluntarily follow and respond to direction from a leader who is authentic and who cares about them.

Meanwhile, the most significant concerns of a fear-based leader are losing control and appearing weak. A fear-based leader needs control points, like an inordinate number of financial and operational reviews, to prop themselves up and create the false appearance of authority.

But is it better to fail and love than to be feared and succeed? This is a question as old as Machiavelli himself. Leaders who don't succeed are losers if and only if they don't take responsibility for their failure and learn from it. The only losers that I have ever met in business are those who refuse to look at themselves in the mirror and accept responsibility for their actions. These are the people who will learn nothing from an experience that likely caused not only them to lose their jobs, but sometimes hundreds or thousands of other people as well.

Employees already know that their leaders have control over their advancement, compensation, and continued employment. Unlike in a love-based culture, people on fear-based teams work to survive rather than to thrive.

To combat encroaching fear, love-based leaders must proactively strip back the personal shell that keeps them from interacting and connecting with employees on a real and human basis. By allowing themselves to be seen as vulnerable, they encourage those they manage to do the same, thereby gaining an even more in-depth understanding of the members of their teams and the value they bring to the table.

The mark of a real leader is someone who doesn't fear being vulnerable. Vulnerability creates an authentic human connection, which builds trust—the foundation of a love-based culture. By allowing yourself to be seen as vulnerable, you encourage those you manage to do the same.

With this in mind, what kind of love, respect, and guidance do you show the employees you work with? It doesn't matter if you're a team leader, the CEO, or a frontline worker. You have an obligation to show up and deliver your best every day.

I have a great "for instance" to share with you. I had a client who did me a favor by getting me on the agenda for a national meeting of Blue Cross Blue Shield CIOs. The meeting started early on a Monday morning, so I flew into town that Sunday.

> Leaders who don't succeed are losers if and only if they don't take responsibility for their failure and learn from it.

Around the same time as this national meeting, my team had hired a new administrative assistant for me, but I had not met her yet. Instead, I let her fellow administrative assistants who knew me well handle the hiring. This new assistant had worked in the office for a few days the previous week, during which time I had been on the road.

As executives, we become victims of our calendars and especially of whomever manages them. Like lemmings, we go where we're told to go and stay where we're told to stay. On this Sunday, I headed to the airport to fly to Indianapolis. I arrived late, grabbed a taxi, and gave the driver the name of my hotel. He paused and said that there were no hotels by that name in Indianapolis.

"What!?" I gasped. I rifled through my calendar and realized that my brand-spanking-new administrator had flown me to the wrong city. I needed to be in Cincinnati, more than 100 miles away. There were no more flights out that night, all rental car agencies were closed, and there were no flights out in the morning that would get me to my meeting on time. I was screwed.

At this point, the taxi driver said, "I can drive you." It was 120 miles door to door. I asked for the price. "Two hundred and fifty dollars."

"Deal!" I said.

The driver stopped to pick up his son so he could have some company (besides me) for the long drive, and I lay out in the back of the taxi to get some sleep. We pulled into my hotel around three o'clock in the morning, and I was at my meeting by seven.

Of course, then I had to go back to the office and find out how my new administrative assistant could have made such a mistake. Again, we'd never met, so I walked through the lobby, down the hall, and into my office. A few minutes later, a tiny woman walked in; she was my new administrative assistant. I looked at her, she looked at me, and then she burst into tears. My heart broke.

At that point, any "lesson" I had wanted to impart to her flew out the window. I gave her a hug and told her not to worry about it. Those real tears told me that she understood what a serious error she had made. The honesty of her emotions made me feel certain that nothing like that would ever happen again.

All's well that ends well. Everything would be fine, I told her, and I was happy that she was on board.

As a leader, are you vulnerable and forgiving? Or do you sulk over to your office or cubicle and hope that no one talks to you all day? If the latter describes you, there's always time to change. Habits are nothing more than repeated behaviors, and those behaviors can be modified. You can unlearn the patterns that have been detrimental to you or to those you lead.

It is possible that you have a blind spot about the way you're showing up; a lot of people do. (Once again, this is where 360-degree feedback helps, though you can also solicit feedback from a trusted associate who isn't afraid to deliver bad news.) Don't forget that you have a choice to demonstrate the highest level of love in your leadership each and every day. Even when those around you don't act or speak with love, you can. Be the example of the change you'd like to see in your teammates and in those you lead.

If you want to create a love-based culture, you either need to be an inherently selfless leader or be ready for a personal transformation that will obliterate your ego and desire for recognition, praise, and fame. You will need to deprogram the years of propaganda about how companies should be run—companies in which chronic stress prevails and winning is defined only by your individual performance rather than the value that you add to the greater good.

Leading With Transparency

Hand in hand with vulnerability comes transparency. John Gribi, the former chief financial officer (CFO) of Compaq Computers and member of Healthlink's board of directors, once told me that every employee needs to be encouraged to say two things: "I need help" and "I don't know." Those are words of wisdom. Creating an atmosphere in which people of all levels, including executives, can say either set of three magical words may well be the ultimate goal of a love-based culture.

How comfortable a company's employees are with being open, transparent, and asking for help may be the single biggest differentiator between a love-based culture and one based in fear, but in my case, I didn't know I needed help until it was too late.

> If you want to create a love-based culture, you either need to be an inherently selfless leader or be ready for a personal transformation that will obliterate your ego and desire for recognition, praise, and fame.

Soon after IBM acquired Healthlink[4], my level of responsibility as a leader changed. My new job involved overseeing the company's healthcare provider businesses all over the world. Between these responsibilities and other tasks IBM asked me to perform, I was overseas, often for weeks at a time. I once hit eight countries during a two-week blitz. On another occasion, I made a day trip to Beijing. When my car would pull up at home, only to leave again 24 to 48 hours later, I would spend my weekends trying to recover in preparation for the next trip.

During this time, my relationship with my wife, Sally, who also had a very demanding job as a hospital executive, was deteriorating. I found myself tired and angry most days when I was home. I was burned out and unhappy. As an entrepreneur, working for a multibillion-dollar company was a miserable experience. I wasn't wired to be a cog in a big wheel. I wasn't used to not being able to make quick decisions. I wasn't used to justifying every move I made. I wasn't used to being told which hotel I could stay in and which route I would take to get to my destination. I certainly wasn't used to having a boss.

I suspect that most people reading this book have experienced the feeling of stress and tension that grows between you and your spouse or significant other when you come home from a business trip. When you have stress at work and stress at home, breathing becomes a challenge.

In March 2007, Sally and I got divorced. My daughter was 13 at the time, so I bought a house within golf-cart-driving distance of Sally's so that the split would minimally impact my daughter. I hired a decorator and gave her a blank check to create an insta-home so that my daughter and I could be comfortable. There was new carpet, new paint, new furniture, and brand-new accessories on shelves around the house, but none of it meant anything to me. It was all just stuff that filled the space.

After yet another week of global travel, I drove into my driveway on a Friday night and entered my new home. I could smell the new carpet. The maid had come, so the house was crisp and clean. My daughter was with her mom, so I was home alone. It was deathly quiet. I looked around, though, and didn't feel that I had come "home." I could see my ex-wife's house from across a field. That was my home.

Then, an overwhelming feeling engulfed me. The feeling was so powerful that I can still feel it today. I was consumed with sadness and literally fell to my knees in tears. I had everything a man could ever want: a beautiful home, a nice car, and money to buy anything I wanted. I had won the most highly coveted business award for entrepreneurs and almost every other leadership award offered in the healthcare IT space. Everyone returned my phone calls. It was in that moment, sobbing like a baby in my shiny, new home, that I realized...

I had everything, yet I had NOTHING.

While I worked harder than at any time in my life, while I learned a great deal about the global business environment, IBM ultimately wasn't a good fit for me. I didn't feel any love from my superiors, peers, or anybody else in the company. There was not enough emotional trust between me and my leadership or employees in order for me to be transparent about my needs during this challenging time. I couldn't share with them the stressors that were plaguing me at home, at work, and on the road, mostly because they, too, were operating in survival mode.

VOICE OF DANA

A key responsibility of leadership is to anticipate problems and act. I know that I made hundreds of mistakes during my years of management, but one of the biggest happened after a long period of very successful growth. I had become used to seeing our business grow month after month.

Then, a little blip came. We had a bad month. I blew it off. I said, "It's just an anomaly. Nothing to worry about. Next month we'll be back on track." But the next month we had problems, too. Again, I thought things had to turn around. I couldn't comprehend that something was fundamentally different. For several months, I made excuses. "That big project got delayed, but things will be back on track as soon as it starts," or "I can't believe we didn't win that proposal, but I'm sure it was just one of those things."

For months, I sat with my head in the sand, denying reality. Finally, though, I had to acknowledge that I was wrong. We had gone astray. I had become complacent, overly confident, and blinded to the fact that I needed to make changes.

It was hard, but I had to own up and let the whole company know that we had a problem. I finally shared the tough financial truth, took responsibility, and asked for help. Just like that, the company came together to solve the problem. We brainstormed ideas and settled on a series of changes that got us back on track.

Transparency is incredibly powerful. Our team was amazing, but they couldn't help me fix anything until they knew we had a problem. By recognizing and communicating openly about the problem, taking responsibility, and asking for help, I was able to bring the power of our whole team to turn the company around.

Leading With Forgiveness

There are corporate cultures that dissuade us from being transparent, but there are also corporate cultures that surprise us by showing the greatest form of authenticity: their forgiveness.

A few years ago, I had an idea for a business that I was convinced would go viral and produce a billion-dollar company. This idea required new software and some innovative services. A multimillion-dollar investment would be needed just to launch this company, so I drove up to Dallas to have dinner with and pitch the deal to Mort Meyerson. He immediately liked the idea and committed a large sum of money as an investment.

To make a long story short, the idea didn't work. I flat-out failed despite my exhaustive efforts.

I vividly recall that one afternoon, I was returning home from business travel. I was waiting for a flight in Denver when my phone rang. I looked at the screen and saw the caller ID identifying Mort. I felt terrible about losing his money; it felt like I had flushed it down the toilet.

This was my first flat-out failure in business, and I was struggling to accept that fact. What was worse, I felt awful for letting down someone who had invested in my idea mostly because of his trust in me.

I answered the phone and said, "Hi, Mort."

The voice on the other end said, "Hey, Ivo. I'm just checking to see how you're doing."

I immediately launched into business mode and talked about how I was working hard to make the deal work, blah, blah, blah, blah.

Mort cut me off mid-sentence and said, "I'm calling to see how Ivo is doing. How are you holding up?"

My jaw hit the floor. I had just wasted millions of dollars of this guy's money, and he wanted to know if I was okay?

After I told him that I was stressed but fine, we had a pleasant conversation. I hung up and took a deep breath. That was love in action.

> I didn't take any classes in college on how to handle success or failure. There was nothing in the curriculum that referred to self-love, to being authentic and transparent, or to forgiveness.

I have sat on corporate and advisory boards; invested with venture capital firms; and run companies with angel, venture, and institutional investors, but I have no words to describe what that conversation with Mort meant to me. Had the call come from some 28-year-old investor who had never run a business before and whose only tool was fear, the tone would have been harsh with an intent to shame me or to kick my ass in a feeble attempt at motivation. Had I received that kind of call, I probably would have shut the company down, minimized my losses, licked my wounds, and moved on.

Mort's call had the opposite effect. He left me feeling motivated and wanting to make this company succeed even more than I had before. My commitment to him personally and to the business went up tenfold. I hunkered down and worked even harder; I downsized and refocused the company.

With his implicit forgiveness, Mort showed love. He didn't have to make that call, but he did, and that brief conversation left an impression on me that I'll never forget. Because Mort showed that he cared about me personally, I found the strength to work even harder. I'm now optimistic that this company, still in the works, is going to hit a grand slam and be a great deal for both of us.

This is the stuff they don't teach in universities. I didn't take any classes in college on how to handle success or failure. There was nothing in the curriculum that referred to self-love, to being authentic and transparent, or to forgiveness. The same is true for corporate training programs. Most true leaders, though, eventually come to the realization that who they really are defines them as a leader—the authentic version of themselves, not the person hiding behind a veneer molded by a culture of rubber stamps.

HOW TO BECOME A LOVE-BASED LEADER

In addition to the four elements that make up authentic, love-based leadership, I hope you'll implement the following practical pieces of advice for becoming a love-based leader.

Taking in 360-Degree Feedback

If you feel that you struggle with or lack self-awareness, I hope you'll find encouragement in the fact that your self-awareness can improve with practice. One of the best ways I know of to improve self-awareness is to participate in 360-degree feedback. As suggested earlier, this is a performance review process in which those all around an employee provide feedback on their performance.

> Most true leaders, though, eventually come to the realization that who they really are defines them as a leader—the authentic version of themselves, not the person hiding behind a veneer molded by a culture of rubber stamps.

Much like the open-door policy we'll discuss in chapter 8, feedback participants should not face retribution for anything that is said during this time. However, they should also understand that this is a time of building up through constructive criticism, not tearing down or throwing under the bus, as often happens in a fear-based culture.

This system works well at increasing self-awareness because it feels less like a mandate on high than traditional "top-down feedback" does, and for this reason, we feel empowered to tackle any weak points. Moreover, by being vulnerable and trusting those around us to provide honest, constructive feedback, we increase the bonds of teamwork we can enjoy at work.

The biggest mistake I see people make with 360-degree feedback is relying too heavily on the feedback they get from peers instead of having an authentic and candid conversation about performance with the employee in question. It's easy to attribute negative feedback to the almighty "them," rather than saying, "I agree, and I need you to know." In cases where you agree with negative feedback in a 360-degree appraisal, treat your suggestions as being validated by the employee's peers, while still coming directly from you.

I also have found it useful to have no rules around who should be included in the feedback. Traditionally, this is a peer review, but I have frequently reached out to clients and to people from all levels inside and outside of an organization. I did this because I wanted to make sure I had as complete a picture of the person I was appraising as was possible. In these cases, there is no such thing as too much information.

Aim To Be Respected, Not To Be Liked

Everyone wants to be liked, but there's a fine line between being a people pleaser and being the strong manager that everyone loves. Leadership is not about being liked, nor is pleasing people every day integral to having a love-based culture.

The best employees want to be a part of a company that sets the bar high, especially when it comes to delivering for customers. Customers have expectations and, frequently, critical timelines. Employees who don't fit on a team that is responsible for achieving these goals need to know where they stand. Sometimes they need to be moved out of the way. They may not feel the love when that happens, but the rest of the team will.

I've had more than one person swear they would never work for me again, only to submit their résumé the next time I started up a company.

On one occasion, an employee who was also a friend of mine resigned. When I asked him why, he said, "You guys are all flying fighter jets. I'm a B-52 bomber. Slow and steady; I don't do fast."

This employee wasn't mad or upset in any way, or even disappointed. He ended up working for the company twice over the course of his career, and we're still great friends. However, he was self-aware and knew where he fit and where he didn't.

VOICE OF DANA

I found it humorous that our employees saw me as the understanding corporate mother who would listen and show empathy, while Ivo was the aggressive, uncompromising driver who had little patience for people's excuses. The fact was that I was the engineer who demanded discipline in processes while Ivo did everything physically possible to connect with every employee in the company as often as possible.

Some people like the fast pace of a young and growing entrepreneurial company, while some are better suited to a more methodical pace. My Love/Fear Continuum sometimes swung wildly between love and fear as I attacked an industry in which I sorely wanted to win. I had the prerogative, as CEO, to establish the pace for the company just as my employees had the prerogative to decide if Healthlink was where they wanted to work. Most importantly, though, I needed to know when fear or speed was temporarily necessary and how soon I could return to managing by love.

Please Secure Your Own Mask Before Assisting Others

Being the leader of a love-based organization means that you need to show love for yourself—your mental, physical, and spiritual wellbeing—so that you can care for all the people who are counting on you: your fellow managers, your employees, your customers, and your investors.

Staying physically, mentally, and emotionally healthy is critical to business leadership. Committing to healthy eating and getting a proper amount of sleep and exercise not only makes you feel better but is important for everyone around you, too. Few people can survive the rigors of weekly flights, living in hotels, late-night eating and drinking, and lack of sleep for any length of time and still be great business leaders. Your team wants and needs a motivated, energetic leader, but you can't be that without making yourself a priority.

Self-love means taking care of yourself. It's different from self-esteem, which is based on how you value yourself, and from self-confidence, which refers to how assured you are that you will perform well. Depending upon other people's approval is dangerous for business leaders. Instead of making sound, independent judgments, a leader dependent upon others' approval may feel an overwhelming inclination to rely on what everybody else thinks and does. That muddles intelligent thoughts and feelings. Self-love, however, allows you to make an emotional connection with yourself before considering any achievements or success.

I asked some of my peers if they had any tips regarding self-love. The responses ranged from attending a spiritual ceremony to going to the spa for a massage. Others just wanted some alone time or a quiet night out with a loved one and no kids. The responses were so varied that I realized self-love must be customized to the person.

As a leader I could sometimes recognize when someone was crossing a line and on the verge of burnout. If I caught it early enough, I could help. In one case I sent one of my executives on a two-week cruise that was so far off the grid she couldn't make phone calls or check email. She needed to disconnect, and that Act of Love did the trick.

There were other times when I didn't pick up on the signals early enough, so that by the time I tried to intervene it was too late, and I lost a good employee. Most people are too proud to ask for help when they're feeling overwhelmed. Often, whatever is going on at work is being compounded by problems at home. When all that pressure comes to a head, good people quit. They quit their jobs. They get divorced. They just need out. The signals are usually obvious if you are listening.

This quitting may sound familiar, after the story I shared of my time at IBM and my divorce. The moral of my story is that every leader needs to take care of himself or herself if they are going to be successful in running their company and caring about the health and wellbeing of their employees and colleagues. I had failed at this most important job because I neglected to pay attention to what was most important in my life—the love of my family—and no amount of money, awards, or accolades could substitute for that.

There is no answer to work/life balance. Only you know where to draw the line. It's naïve to think that successful businesses are built by people who work nine-to-five jobs. Take your eye off the ball for even a second, and hungry competitors will eat your lunch. There will be times in your career when you need to push hard and times when you need to back off. Only you will know the difference.

For some people, maintaining this balance may involve reducing the number of hours they spend at work, while for others, the only thing that needs to change is being aware of what's important and never taking it for granted.

I'm lucky in that I recognized my problem and set about restoring the proper balance in my life. Once I grasped that, I worked to reverse the rotation of the earth and give myself a chance to win Sally back. At that moment, I would have given back the wealth I had accumulated to have my family back. As I was weeping on the floor in the middle of my living room, I realized I had made a mistake. I wanted to go home.

Hang with me here, because it's this next part of the story that will make your day.

I had a tiny problem as I started planning my return. My wife had moved on. She had grieved our separation and divorce, but had since met someone she liked. It wasn't a serious relationship yet, but it was clearly heading that way. So, I had some competition. I realized that my primary objective was to get her to fall in love with me all over again. That would not be easy for either of us after recently experiencing the pain of divorce.

I knew that if I really was going to put my family first, I had to get out of the rat race I was in, so I quit my job at IBM. IBM had been more than fair to me, but I needed to get my health back. I needed to stop taking sleeping pills to deal with jet lag, exercise occasionally, eat healthy meals, and regularly get a full night's sleep. I knew that if I wasn't healthy physically, I could never give what I needed to emotionally.

With that, I kicked off the best marketing campaign I've ever executed. I started by sitting down with Sally and letting her know that I had made a mistake and wanted her to consider starting over again. While the divorce was a mutual decision, she had been hurt and still felt the pain. I needed to refresh her memory of the good times rather than grovel in the misery of the dark days.

To do this, I bought blank greeting cards, and filled them with handwritten love notes, each featuring a memory from the past. I left the cards on her windshield at work, where she was the CEO of the local hospital. Every day when she got off work and went to her car, there would be a card. Every day. When I knew she would be traveling, I'd mail a card to her hotel so she could still read a memory from me. I didn't want a day to go by without her feeling something positive about us.

I finally asked Sally out on a date, and when I showed up at the front door with a big bouquet of roses, she burst into tears. It was like we had met and fallen in love all over again. In December, nine months after our divorce, we remarried, and we have stayed very happily married ever since.

This experience, while incredibly difficult, taught me a valuable lesson. I had given everything to my company and very little to my family. I can't get that time back; it's gone. I didn't understand the concept of self-love and surely didn't appreciate the fact that if I couldn't take care of myself, I certainly wouldn't be able to help others. If I couldn't find balance of any kind in my life, then I had no life. At least not the kind of life most people value.

For the most part, we live in a suck-it-up world in which any sign of weakness is considered the first step toward failure. The last thing I would have done at IBM, when I was at my lowest point, would have been to raise my hand and ask for help. I was so determined to prove to the world that I could succeed in any environment, working for any company, at any level, that I lost track of me. That is not a knock on IBM, but rather a testament to my inability to find balance. I never even gave IBM the chance to help.

Leadership starts with YOU. Too many leaders in business today are a byproduct of the fear-based cultures in which they started their careers. At the same time, though, they feel out of their element in a fear-based culture because that's not who they are. It's not how they were raised; it's not how they operate anywhere in their lives except at work. These business leaders have allowed their workplace's fear-based culture to tell them who to be. If this describes you, I encourage you to look within and return to the natural you. Yes, even at the office.

Be the leader your mom wants you to be.

PRINCIPLE #2

LEADERSHIP
Put Your Employees' Needs Ahead of Your Own

While a love-based leader needs to execute for their company by using solid business fundamentals, what differentiates them from their fear-based counterparts is simple: they care. Love-based leaders put their employees' needs above their own. However, love-based leaders know that in order to be of service to their customers and employees, they first must be and emotionally healthy themselves.

Call to Action:

» Do you trust that the leadership of your company is looking out for your best interests first and themselves second?

» Do you believe your leaders create a safe and secure environment for you and your peers?

» Do you feel comfortable being transparent, vulnerable, and asking for help when you need it at work?

» How can you achieve greater self-awareness in the future?

» Can you take the high road and forgive those who are using corporate politics for self-promotion?

» Can you be the same loving person at work as you are at home, with friends, or in the community you serve?

My Lessons Learned:

» There are no standard rules for work/life balance. Each of us is in a different place in life. Each of us has different tolerances for stress. Each of us has different career ambitions. You must be aware of the balance you need to thrive in the long term and develop a program that works for you.

» Fewer than 15% of people are self-aware. If you think that you are one of those 15%, you are probably mistaken. Find a friend and get some honest feedback, regardless of how painful that "look in the mirror" might be.

» If you rationalize failure with any of the "dog ate my homework" excuses that can be used for failed businesses, then you are a loser. Take responsibility and see failure as a learning opportunity. Then you will likely win over and over again in the future.

ACTS OF LOVE

A consultant was part of a large team that worked together in Dallas, Texas. She flew into town every week and was a highly reliable, hardworking member of the team.

One day, though, she did not show up to the client site. The team got worried and called her. She said she was ill, that she had a horrible headache. The team went to check on her and found that she was clearly having neurological symptoms. They made calls, and she was immediately admitted to a local hospital, where the staff found a cancerous brain tumor.

Things went downhill quickly. Three days after her hospital admission, the consultant could not remember her laptop password. The company flew her family to Dallas, but the consultant wanted to go home and be treated there. The company and her team rallied around her, contributing airline miles, etc., to get her and her family back home.

Once she was home, the company and her team continued to provide the consultant with support and care. Unfortunately, the cancer was not treatable, and the consultant passed away. However, her family was so grateful for the support and care shown by the company that her son nominated the company for *Modern Healthcare's* "Best Places to Work."

3

CORE VALUES:
Be Uncompromising in Living Core Values Daily

It's remarkable what you can learn from nuns. When I served on a board of directors' committee for CHRISTUS Health, a large, faith-based healthcare system in Texas, I realized how important values can be to an organization. While the sisters no longer ran CHRISTUS Health as its CEOs, their presence still loomed large over the board, specifically to remind everyone of the mission they served in improving the health of their communities.

The first meeting I attended opened with a "reflection." This meant that one of the board members read a beautiful poem, which we discussed before starting the meeting. Beginning the meeting with our intention focused on a greater good had a huge impact on me.

I returned to Healthlink's offices and told my executive team that we were going to start every meeting with a discussion of our core values. This would make the importance of our values real to all of the company's managers. Someone would pick a value, and we would discuss what it meant, reviewing examples of where we had succeeded or sometimes failed to manifest that value over the past week. Those conversations turned out to be honest and transparent, and had the clear intent of making us authentic as an executive team in our desire to do what was right for the customers we served. We kept it real, and we kept the values alive.

The honesty and respect that we, as senior managers, showed for our values flowed throughout the organization. The process kept us honest as a team. Anyone in the company, no matter their position, could call out a behavior that wasn't consistent with our values. I never found those discussions to involve threats, finger-pointing, or criticism. We truly wanted to live our values, and those conversations were instrumental in keeping us focused.

PRINCIPLE #3
CORE VALUES
Be Uncompromising in Living Core Values Daily

By having a set of core values in your love-based culture, you create a battle flag that all of your employees can rally around. For instance, though Dana and I had opposite management styles, we were always aligned around the same values. Those shared values went a long way toward creating a love-based culture at Healthlink.

Business leaders who want to embrace a love-based culture need to believe in their hearts that they will run their company in accordance with its values. This creates the filter through which every decision will flow. It goes beyond self-less leadership and is proactive in creating an environment in which everyone feels protected, safe, and invested in the work they perform.

In its 2013 report, "State of the Global Workplace: Employee Engagement Insights for Business Leaders Worldwide," Gallup found that across 142 countries, only 13% of the workforce studied was emotionally invested or "engaged" in their work.[1] A full 63% of workers were "not engaged" while an additional 24% percent were "actively disengaged."

Engagement matters. According to another study, "Engaged employees are 3.5 times more likely than disengaged employees to do something good for the company that is unexpected of them, 3.5 times more likely to make a recommendation about an improvement, and 5.8 times more committed to helping their organization succeed."[2] Imagine if all these employees had been engaged in their work! That's what love and core values can do for you.

In fact, if your core values become an integral part of your internal culture, then they will also evolve to become part of your external reputation within your industry vertical, all because your employees believe in these tenets and live them day in and day out.

HEALTHLINK'S VALUES

Company values are hung up around most offices, but how many people really pay attention to them instead of treating them as empty words? How many companies have value statements that say one thing, while the leadership style and supporting processes say another? If the values plastered on the walls in your conference rooms promote teamwork yet your compensation policies reward individual goals, then those framed value statements become meaningless.

At Healthlink, our team, our company, our customers, and our commitment to quality formed the framework of our core values. These values changed over time with our markets, products, and size, so every few years we'd form a team that engaged many employees at once to provide input on these values.

What was important was that our employees owned these values and that we as business leaders walked the talk. Team members will become as committed to the company as leadership is when they see the organization's core values in action.

The values we established at Healthlink were the foundation of our company's culture and the standard by which we conducted business. They outlined how our teams should instinctively incorporate these values into their professional lives and decision-making processes. Values can change as a company grows. Markets change, and we learned from those experiences what our industry's culture demanded of us.

The following were the specific elements of our core values. Perhaps you can use them as a launching point to build your own.

Our Team

We believe that our team is our greatest asset. We foster an environment that encourages open, honest, and sincere communication. No surprises allowed. We are each accountable for Healthlink's success. We seek input and guidance from each other.

- Treat others with respect and dignity.
- Communicate. Communicate. Communicate.
- Promote teamwork and integrity.
- Accept mutual accountability.
- Embrace diversity.

Our Company

We believe each individual's experiences, talents, knowledge, and efforts contribute to the overall success of our company.

- Never compromise on excellence.
- Attract and retain top talent.
- Run the business as if it's your own.
- Encourage innovation.

Our Customers

We believe in doing what is right for the customer. We deliver added value to our customers. We act with the highest levels of integrity and honesty. We actively listen to our customers.

- Protect customers' interests and confidentiality.
- Effect positive change.
- Do what it takes to make our customers successful.

Our Commitment to Quality

We believe in never compromising on quality. Our standard is 100% referenceability.

- Deliver proven performance and guaranteed results.
- Challenge the process.
- Provide best practice solutions.

DO YOU KNOW YOUR COMPANY'S VALUES?

While corporations frequently offer classes on "culture" in their leadership training programs, their employees are often disappointed when they get into the real world and learn that the company's policies, procedures, and processes don't support the core principles they've committed to memory.

Prior to giving a keynote speech at a recent conference, I researched the companies that would be attending the conference and identified the two largest. I went to their websites and copied their published values into my PowerPoint presentation. I did not identify the companies associated with each list of values, but when I got to that part of the presentation, I asked the audience if anyone recognized which companies the values belonged to. I waited. Not a single hand went up. No one in the room recognized that the values listed on the screen were from their own company.

VOICE OF DANA

You may be the owner of a start-up thinking, 'That sounds great, but how do I define what my company's core values will be?'

For us, it was a simple process. One day, the little team that started up what became Healthlink found itself in a car with some time together. My colleague Dave grabbed a pad of paper, and we posed this brainstorming question: "What are the core values that we want to live by in our new company?"

As we drove, we went around the car, with each person offering a thought to add to the list. There were no rules; anything was fair game. The only stipulation was that we couldn't name something that had already been said. Dave captured each idea verbatim as we went.

When we ran out of ideas, the next step was to "affinitize" the list, or group like items together. As we came up with a group of like items, we gave it a name, like "running a good business."

After giving the list a thoughtful edit to add anything we'd missed and to remove things that didn't fit, the team gave the list its final blessing.

Then, the challenge became finding ways to make sure we lived by the list. We created core-value cards for employees' wallets, we created a graphic to show the core values, and we drew up standard PowerPoint slides to explain our values to employees and to our customers. A whole section on core values became part of every new employee's orientation. We gave awards to employees who best exemplified our core values. We even incorporated our core values into our ranking discussions and our employee reviews. At retreats, our core values were always given top billing.

Our core values were important to us and didn't change dynamically, but periodically we'd form a team of employees to do a refresh.

Our core values worked because we committed ourselves to keeping them front and center.

I remember one specific time that I was deeply moved by how much our employees believed in our values. Business was down in one area, and we had to let a few people go. One of the people who was let go asked to speak to me. I thought maybe he was mad or wanted to plead his case. Instead, he simply said that he believed in our core value of "running a good business" and understood and respected our decision. He said he hoped he could come back one day if the situation changed. What a testament to our core values!

★ ★ ★

DEVELOPING YOUR COMPANY'S CORE VALUES: A STARTER KIT

If you need help brainstorming your own list of core values, you might be able to implement the following examples into your own company.

The Customer Always Comes First

As stated in chapter 1, chief among Healthlink's values was an uncompromising commitment to our customers. Our HR policies, compensation programs, and core processes were all designed to accommodate a culture that put customers first. As part of this undertaking within the healthcare industry, we were fortunate that many of our employees were nurses, doctors, and other medical professionals who appreciated that we could really make a difference in patient care.

Whenever any of our managers asked for direction on a touchy situation, all we had to do was remind them to "do what's right." As a result, short-term quarterly results took a distant second place to long-term customer satisfaction.

Our commitment to making customers happy drove everything we did. We knew that we needed to hire and retain the very best people to achieve a tough goal like that, so we made sure to treat our people well and create a great place to work. Processes like teamwork and training were critical and supported by tools that captured product experiences so we didn't have to reinvent the wheel for every customer. All our thinking and investments centered on the lofty goal of having a 100%-referenceable customer base.

Did we ignore the bottom line? No. We knew we had to run a good business and we had a responsibility to our shareholders, so we put good business processes and practices in place. We never let profit concerns override our goal of having 100%-referenceable customers. When a project was in trouble, we accepted that our profits might suffer, but a short-term loss was acceptable in the interest of long-term gain.

> Whenever any of our managers asked for direction on a touchy situation, all we had to do was remind them to "do what's right."

Embrace A Different Way Of Doing Business

One day as I was sitting at my desk, I got a call from Bruce, an IT executive at Kaiser Permanente of California, the largest healthcare system in the U.S. It was larger, even, than most countries' entire health systems. I had been trying to get a foot in the door at Kaiser for years, and now I had THE MAN on the phone.

Bruce told me that Kaiser was on the front end of a massive IT project and needed help. He had been asking around and had landed on two companies. We were one of them. "I want you to come out here next week," he said, "so I can get to know you and a few of your people." Though I drooled over the prospect of landing this big elephant of a customer, Bruce threw me a ringer when I asked him what I should prepare. He repeated, "I want to get to know you and your team. Please don't bring a PowerPoint presentation."

This was a first. Just show up and chat? No pitch? I gathered a few people, and off we went to meet Bruce in Oakland,

California. We had an engaging discussion on healthcare, methodologies, our approach, and so on. Our team did a great job at the whiteboard, drawing methodologies and process maps and showcasing their experience. We asked questions and listened intently to Bruce's issues so we could understand the scope of the project.

At one point he asked one of our employees, "So, why do you work for Healthlink?"

Her reply was genuine. "I've worked as a clinician in this industry for 25 years, and I want to make a difference. I know I can do that working here."

After the meeting, we headed home. A few days later, Bruce called and told me we had won the contract. Naturally, I was delighted, but I also wanted to know what had helped him make his decision. He said that we had shown up, had an authentic conversation, and shown honesty. Then he specifically mentioned our nurse who wanted to make a difference. We were the kind of people he wanted to work with on a project that he knew would be a challenge in an organization as large and complex as Kaiser. He also mentioned that, in contrast, our competitor had flown in on a private jet, worn expensive suits and shiny black shoes, and come prepared with an impressive laser-light show — everything he didn't want. We, however, had listened.

Keep Your Promises

Customers knew Healthlink as the firm that would always do what it promised. At one hospital in Missouri, some members of the project team lacked chemistry with the customer. The team wasn't working well together, and the project was in trouble. The hospital's CIO was concerned and called the executive whose job it was to oversee the quality of work being done on this account. The Healthlink account executive immediately flew to the customer site and told the CIO that he would get the project back on track and stay there until it was accomplished.

Before the end of the day, the problem employees were identified, removed from the account, and sent back to their hotel rooms. Then the account manager had conversations with other members of the team to identify who was both qualified to do the work and a good fit for this specific customer's culture. The other employees were redeployed to other projects where they would have a better chance at success. Within a matter of days, new team members were introduced to the customer and the handoff was complete. In fewer than 72 hours, the CIO saw a dramatic response to his problem, which undoubtedly made him even more committed to choosing us as his vendor.

In cases like this, we would evaluate whether the issues were due to certain employees not performing well. If so, we needed to assess whether they had made some one-off mistake or whether they had a history of problems that required either counseling or a possible exit from the company. Sometimes, it was our fault: we had done a lousy job of matching people to projects and customers, in which case there was a lesson to be learned on our part. In all cases, we learned and adjusted.

Love Having Fun

While business can be challenging in the heat of competition, there's a soft side that needs to be recognized and highlighted with a million bright lights. It's that soft side that will inspire employees to go the extra mile and work to improve the overall value of the company.

So, where does flat-out having fun fit into a company's core values? Not surprisingly, it may well be the most important part of a healthy love-based culture.

In the 1980s, Edward Deci and Richard Ryan conducted a study at the University of Rochester in which they identified the six main reasons why people work: play, purpose, potential, emotional pressure, economic pressure, and inertia.[3]

Play, purpose, and potential all evoke higher-level emotions. Emotional pressure, economic pressure, and inertia do not. This makes sense if you consider the joy you experience when you are having fun at work (play) or feel like your work is connected to a higher calling (purpose) and can see a bright future for your career (potential).

Now, contrast that with people who work because they want to avoid disappointing themselves or others (emotional pressure), work only to make money to pay the bills (economic pressure), or get up every day and grind it out because that's what they did the day before and the day before (inertia).

Though this study was conducted in the 1980s, the conclusions have held true over the decades. In a 2012 paper, "The Fundamental Role of Workplace Fun in Applicant Attraction," Michael J. Tews, John W. Michel, and A.L. Bartlett noted that "Fun may be particularly relevant during difficult economic times... where employees are being asked to do more for less."[4] The study included students from 3 large universities who had an average age of 22 years old.

> Common sense tells us that a corporate culture in which people like their jobs, like their boss, and love operating in the spirit of teamwork is going to promote happiness, health, and prosperity.

These students were randomly assigned to read ads for a hypothetical management trainee position. The content of the ads was mixed, so that only some included a description of a fun work environment, competitive compensation plan, and advancement opportunities.

This led the researchers to conclude that, for Millennials, workplace fun has just as strong of a pull as compensation and advancement opportunities. "A job ad that touts fun among a company's core values," adds Kathy Gurchiek for the Society for Human Resource Development, "with references to a welcoming, cohesive environment, meaningful work, and entertaining activities during and after work—may be a valuable tool."[5]

Here are a few things companies can do to create fun in the workplace that sets them apart from their competitors:

- GoDaddy puts money toward offsite employee activities held during work hours. These have included panning for gold, whitewater rafting, trapeze classes, and competitive cooking courses.

- Pike Place Fish Market in Seattle has workers who fling fish, use corny puns, and perform CPR on fish to the delight of the public.

- Zappos, the online footwear company, has staff members perform *Saturday Night Live*-style skits during new hire orientations.

- Salesforce provides up to seven days of paid leave for employees to volunteer in their community.

- Patagonia offers flextime based on weather conditions so employees can go surfing when the waves are gnarly or skiing when there's fresh powder.

- Zynga makes every day a "Bring Your Dog to Work" day and offers pet insurance, a rooftop dog park, and treats for employees' dogs.

- Netflix doesn't track vacation days or work hours. They only measure what people get done.[6]

Having fun at work often results in happy, healthy employees. Common sense tells us that a corporate culture in which people like their jobs, like their boss, and love operating in the spirit of teamwork is going to promote happiness, health, and prosperity.

PUTTING CORE VALUES INTO ACTION

No matter how noble your company's core values, if all they do is hang in an elegant frame on the wall, then they are not assisting you in your love-based mission.

Whether you've just drafted your first set of core values or they've been printed on the first page of the employee handbook for decades, I encourage you to examine them. Speak with your managers and your HR team to determine practical, actionable ways you can start walking your talk today.

PRINCIPLE #3

CORE VALUES
Be Uncompromising in Living Core Values Daily

Core values become real when you open every internal meeting with a reflection on one of your values. Start with a brief discussion that demonstrates recent examples of a time when the value worked and when it did not. If you do not frequently revisit your values, they will not be real for your employees.

Call to Action:

» Do you know the core values of your company?

» Do you believe the leaders of your company "walk the talk"? Do you walk the talk?

» Are you involved in a discussion of your company's core values every week?

» Are your core values reviewed and updated periodically as your company grows?

My Lessons Learned:

» Use a cross-section of your company to form teams that will create your core values. The values need to be owned by all the employees. Revisit them with new teams every two years or so. The values will change as the company matures and grows.

» Open every key management meeting with a five-minute discussion of one of your core values. This needs to be an honest discussion in which examples are given of where your value was honored or not followed. There's no other way to keep them alive unless the leadership of the company actively discusses them.

» When values are violated, act swiftly and decisively. It takes years to build trust and one bad decision to lose it.

» Have fun. Be fun. Life's too damn short not to.

ACTS OF LOVE

I was 25 years old and in my first real job at a nationally renowned organization. I had been working day and night to put together the technical response for a large tender that we ultimately won. Immediately thereafter, I was contacted by the assistant of a senior vice president, one of those unapproachable and all-powerful corporate deities held in fear and awe by all the younger employees. She informed me that this vice president wanted me to accompany him on a trip to negotiate with a very large potential customer.

When I arrived at the airport for our flight out, he handed me a first-class ticket to San Francisco. This was my first time not flying in coach. The senior vice president sat next to me on the flight, talking to me about the business and instructing me that, during the customer meeting, I should sit, listen, and take notes.

After the meeting, he took me out to dinner where he simultaneously gave me my first course in wine appreciation and engaged me in a wonderful discussion of the meeting that I had just observed. During dinner, he answered a question that I had posed about a moment in the meeting in which he appeared to argue against our company's interest. He then said something that has stuck with me throughout my entire career: "It is okay to lose business, but never lose a good customer."

4

A HIGHER CALLING:
Have Purpose Beyond Profits

In 2012, John Mackey, CEO and co-founder of Whole Foods, and Raj Sisodia, co-founder and chairman of a nonprofit organization that focuses on "the innate potential of business to make a positive impact on the world,"[1] wrote a book that spawned the idea of conscious capitalism. It focused on the culture, purpose, stakeholder orientation, and leadership of socially conscious businesses. Today, it's hard to read a business article or hear an ad that doesn't somehow touch on the idea of the conscious company, but what does it mean? From the start of the movement in 2012, the term has been used in many different ways.

For their book, *Conscious Capitalism: Liberating the Heroic Spirit of Business*, Mackey and Sisodia studied 28 companies that they felt qualified as socially conscious companies. The ones that followed conscious principles—by having a culture that fosters love, care, and inclusiveness, and that builds trust among the company's team members and all its other stakeholders[2]—outperformed the S&P 500 over a 15-year period.

In fact, according to Deloitte's 2013 Core Beliefs and Culture Survey, having a sense of purpose is associated with a company's long-term financial success.[3] They found that 90% of respondents who felt that their company had a strong sense of purpose also said that their company had performed well over the past year, while 91% felt that their company had a history of strong financial purpose.[4]

PRINCIPLE #4
A HIGHER CALLING
Have Purpose Beyond Profits

As Millennials entered the workforce in the early 2000s, they brought expectations that their employers would be socially responsible and sacrifice profits to support a higher calling.[5] They put their money where their mouths were, too. According to a study by Fidelity, "Millennials would take an average pay cut of $7,600 if they could improve their career development, find more purposeful work, better work-life balance, or a better company culture."[6] This group currently ranges from its early 20s to late 30s, and many of its members have families who are influenced by their career choices. Even so, they expect to exchange money for social accountability, and prefer to support socially responsible companies when spending money.

Increasingly, businesses have begun incorporating the concept of a higher calling into their strategic planning. As they develop business plans and conduct annual strategy sessions, goals such as reducing waste and material consumption, reducing the impact on the environment, and developing healthier and more engaged employees are being integrated into how businesses operate.

This social impact goes beyond your company and extends to your community. If the way your company wants to have a social impact isn't embedded in its core values, this younger generation of employees won't buy in. They will see right through any PR campaign in which your company tries to look cool because of the social impact it advertises.

> ## "Millennials would take an average pay cut of $7,600 if they could improve their career development, find more purposeful work, better work-life balance, or a better company culture."
>
> ### LARRY ALTON

Take Patagonia, for example. The company's mission is to "[b]uild the best product, cause no unnecessary harm, use business to inspire and implement solutions to the environmental crisis."[7] This mission statement drives Patagonia's business decisions. This is a company that walks the talk and is respected by its customers, suppliers, and employees for standing firm in its conviction to do what's right for the environment.

I've talked to several friends who run corporate giving programs. Each has told me that any contribution needs to have an eventual return on investment. One company contributes assets and resources to countries that they want to enter in an attempt to become a "crown jewel." When I worked at IBM, entire countries saw the corporation as a "crown jewel" because of the vast number of philanthropic contributions they made, either in cash or product donations. Investing in a country's education system was part of a long-term strategy to establish the company as an insider that gave rather than an outsider that took. It was clear to me that IBM employees felt proud of their company for performing good deeds.

FINDING A HIGHER PURPOSE IN TEA, FOOD, AND EVEN SHOES

Every company can find its higher calling. While Healthlink had employees who wanted to provide outstanding service while solving healthcare problems, other companies have found their own ways to link their mission and vision to an important calling. For example:

- *Panera Bread's Higher Purpose:* "Provide high-quality, nutritious food with dignity to people in need."[8]

- *Honest Tea's Higher Purpose:* "Create and promote great-tasting, healthy, organic beverages."[9]

- *The Body Shop's Higher Purpose:* "Dedicate our business to the pursuit of social and environmental change."[10]

- *TOMS' Higher Purpose:* "Provide shoes, sight, water, safe birth and bullying prevention services to people in need."[11]

People want to have a higher purpose and be surrounded by peers that have their backs. While being a conscious company can mean being environmentally aware, it has much more to do with creating a culture in which every employee feels like they are a part of a greater good. If that greater good is focused on customers, then all risk of losing business because of abrupt changes in the market, purchasing patterns, or aggressive competitors taking market share is reduced.

A SOCIALLY CONSCIOUS COMPANY IS A LOVE-BASED COMPANY

All of this "conscious company" stuff sounds great, but back when I was a junior businessman, the conscious capitalism movement was still a decade away. I didn't start companies with the idea that I wanted to achieve a higher purpose, but since Healthlink was in the healthcare business, it was natural to think about improving the quality of healthcare. By itself, that was a dominant force in the company, but we moved into hyperdrive when we set a goal of making 100% of our customers referenceable. Together, caring about improving healthcare and committing to 100% referenceability blended into a work environment in which passion, personal pride, integrity, and a desire to be successful all came together. We had created a higher purpose on steroids.

Our goal of being 100% referenceable allowed us to deliver on a higher calling, achieve high employee retention, have robust revenue growth, and recruit new hires of good quality. Our success was due to our uncompromising commitment to being a company that always got it right for our customers.

Rod Canion once told me, "The major thing that separates good business people from great business people is judgment." Basing every decision on what's best for the long-term viability of your business will make you more conscious, whether you realize it or not.

The best way to focus on long-term financial results is to set the bar high for your internal corporate culture and external customer expectations. At Healthlink, we treated our employees with a great deal of respect. They, in turn, worked toward the higher calling of making a difference in patient care, and made sure that those services were delivered at the highest level of quality.

To ensure that this high quality could become a predictable process, not just a flash in the pan, we made a commitment to attract and retain the best and brightest employees. What made us attractive as an employer was that our employees knew we would do anything, including making financial sacrifices, to keep our customers happy. From our board of directors on down, everyone understood that our commitment was never to be compromised. The love-based culture that emerged was a direct byproduct of having a team that believed that achieving individual performance goals was far less important than providing outstanding service to customers.

Healthlink's employees not only wanted to perform work that they believed was meaningful, but also to perform work

Customer-First Focus

that was recognized as the best in the eyes of our customers. They wanted to see "wins" in the sales column because of the quality of service they provided. Their higher calling was to improve patient care, a viable goal because they knew that Healthlink would do everything possible to help them achieve it.

They also knew that, in the heat of battle, the company had their backs. To disappoint a customer was their worst nightmare, and everyone put their reputation on the line when they were at work.

Our employees were on the front lines every day. They were the ones who had to look the customer in the eyes and tell them if there was a problem with a project. No one wanted to do that! In our case, because Healthlink created information technology solutions for some of the country's biggest healthcare systems, there was the added stress that the difference between success and failure could mean the difference between life and death. We dealt with patient care systems, and an error could endanger a patient's life. To our employees, knowing that management was as committed to their success as they were was huge.

Please keep in mind that this was our goal. It was perfect for the services we provided in our industry. If you make shoes, sell toys, practice law, or run movie theaters, 100% referenceability may not be the best goal for you. Instead, you'll need to set your own quality metric. I would encourage you to consider setting one that many believe is not achievable. The gap between what might be easily within reach and what seems unattainable is fear. Don't allow the fear of failure to dictate how high you set the bar. I would not have believed that it was possible to make 100% of our customers referenceable until we did it in our first year.

Conscious companies care about and value their stakeholders, including their customers, their employees, and their community. Their compensation programs reward value. When value is linked to being 100% referenceable, for instance, teams become motivated to work together for the common goal of knocking the ball out of the park for the customer. The team's goal is primary, and individual performance metrics matter only to ensure that expectations are aligned for each employee. These metrics need to be strongly tied to the value the individual achieves in helping the team succeed. This means that employees are more engaged with one another, more loyal to the company, and that customers are happier. How could that not improve a company's bottom line?

> The gap between what might be easily within reach and what seems unattainable is fear.

ARE CONSCIOUS COMPANIES FINANCIALLY TENABLE?

If you're a Millennial, you're probably pretty comfortable with the idea of a conscious company. It feels natural to you. But if you're a baby boomer, you may be reading this and thinking, "WHAT?" The idea of combining capitalism and being "socially conscious" may seem like mixing oil and water. Here's the interesting fact, though: being a conscious company is good for capitalism.

For example, in researching this book, I came across TOMS Shoes.[12] This company is doing amazing things for children around the world, donating a pair of shoes to a child in need for every shoe purchase made by a consumer. They clearly have a higher purpose; however, that higher purpose first requires them to make great shoes. TOMS could not pursue its higher purpose unless they produced a quality product that consumers wanted to purchase.

At Healthlink, we didn't put a second of thought into being a socially responsible, socially conscious, or a doing-well-by-doing-good company. While we understood the importance of considering customers, employees, vendors, and investors as our stakeholders, we weighted customers more highly on our priority list than other stakeholders. While it's easy to state that all stakeholders are important, the fact is that without customers, nothing else really matters.

Some conscious companies have failed because of their uncompromising commitment to creating happy employees, serving the planet, and sticking to values despite markets that don't support them anymore. (There's a reason there are no conscious covered-wagon companies.) It is easy for companies to become so internally focused that they lose touch with what's happening in their external markets. Competitors can swoop in and steal customers while these conscious companies stay busy keeping their employees happy and trying to save the planet.

It's inarguable that both stakeholders and higher callings are important to our society as a whole, but if the customer gets lost in the consciousness shuffle, then there may be no business to serve them, much less a conscious business.

This is less likely to happen in companies that strive to achieve 100% referenceability, which requires an extreme focus on customers and the external markets. When your customer is at the center of your universe, changes in customer priorities, purchasing patterns, competitive pressure, and so on are all noticed early. Any changes occurring in the external markets will be detected by employees and may force quick changes to market strategies.

Companies that work toward 100% referenceability listen intently to what their customers value and deliver that value at an acceptable price. In these companies, communication moves up, down, and across the chain of command at light speed. This is essential to staying ahead of competitive forces.

> While it's easy to state that all stakeholders are important, the fact is that without customers, nothing else really matters.

At Healthlink, we didn't put our people and the needs of the planet above profits; we focused on our customers, understanding that, to be a 100%-referenceable company, our people had to work as a team and feel respected. And when customers are happy, all stakeholders benefit.

NEVER LOSING SIGHT OF YOUR CUSTOMER

For two summers during high school, I drove an ice cream truck in Waco, Texas. That's right, one of those trucks that make the exceedingly loud, obnoxious jingle that sends your kids into a frenzy, asking for whatever change you have in your pocket.

I had the honor of training for this job under the tutelage of "Billy," a legend with Pied Piper Ice Cream, in the 1970s. Billy was a track star at Baylor University and needed to work to finance his education. Billy was the greatest ice cream man ever to walk the earth.

On my first day, as we were driving to our route, Billy explained that success as an ice cream man has everything to do with process, efficiency, and a big, happy smile. As an example, he pointed out that the ice cream truck had no doors. This made it easy to jump out when it was time to sell ice cream and then jump back in en route to the next kid, who was likely a few doors down.

Billy's technique involved turning off the standard-shift engine and jumping out while the truck was still in motion. This bought him valuable time as the truck came to a stop without him in the driver's seat. He positioned himself perfectly at the back of the truck where, with a huge smile (especially for the moms who controlled the coins), he could whip open the door of the freezer and sell popsicles, Fudgsicles, and pints of whatever ice cream a kid or parent desired. He would then jump back into the truck, his feet landing on the clutch and accelerator pedals as his hand turned the ignition back on, all in one smooth motion. Watching Billy was like going to the ballet.

Billy also explained that the timing of the route was crucial. Precise times and turns were listed on index cards that not only determined where to turn left or right, but the precise time to be at a certain corner. Kids knew that, for instance, at 2:23 p.m., the ice cream man would show up on their street. They needed to be out on the curb at that time or there would be no ice cream. If the truck missed this appointment, kids had meltdowns, thus creating ill will from the moms toward the ice cream man. It was therefore crucial to time the route to perfection, in much the same way that NFL wide receivers must be in position to receive a pass thrown by the quarterback.

The two summers I drove the Pied Piper truck taught me lessons that proved invaluable to my business career. I learned that efficiency and discipline (such as not eating your entire inventory) were key to making money. I learned that, despite Billy's ballet, the devil was in the details of successful selling, where time was spent with the customer, not in the entry and exit of the truck.

It doesn't matter if you are a team of 1 or 100, committing to putting the customer first is essential to business success. Making the statement that customers are your most important stakeholders or even implying that all stakeholders aren't equal may be controversial to conscious-company devotees. They will contend that putting employees first creates an environment where customers thrive. That having the best employees and keeping them happy and productive will lead to better products and more customers.

While this could become an academic debate, I'm going to stick to my guns for the simple fact that, in my experience at many companies at multiple stages of business evolution, the one death trap they all fell into was not comprehending the intense focus necessary to attract and retain customers. Many of these happy companies do everything I would expect a conscious company to do, and yet they fail. They fail because they run out of cash due to a lack of revenue from customers.

Hiring great people and treating them right, having a higher calling, giving back to society, and treating the earth with respect are important to the character of a company. You will be a better company if you can check those boxes, but even fear-based, socially unconscious companies can survive and sometimes thrive if they attract and retain customers. Being socially conscious to the detriment of revenue is death.

VOICE OF DANA

I remember a time very early in Healthlink's history when I had a tough customer situation. At the time, we had only two customers, and our revenue was evenly divided between them. An information systems manager at one of our customer's companies asked us to do some programming for them. It was a simple programming change, she explained, but it was urgent and the executive team was in an uproar because there were big, highly visible issues related to a missing field that needed to capture authorization by an insurance company.

Programming wasn't our core competency, but I just happened to have a consultant with the right skills, so I agreed to the project. Our comfort zone was process re-engineering, so before we started programming, we decided to examine the process to be sure we understood what was broken. We held a couple of focus groups to review the process and discovered that the problem was a lot bigger than just adding a field to a screen. In fact, the whole process needed to be revised.

Just as we were finding serious process issues, the customer came to me and said, "Stop wasting time on all these focus groups and start writing code! I need this change now!" She was really unhappy with us. I knew that the "right" thing was to fix both the process and the technology, but it was clear she didn't want to hear that. I was worried that if I refused to proceed with the coding change she'd fire us. The rest of our work for that customer might also be at jeopardy. That reflected half the revenue of the company.

I talked to Ivo about what to do. After listening to my description of the problem, he said simply, "Do what's right." How liberating it was to know that we didn't have to play games or put quarterly metrics above doing the right thing!

I went to the customer and explained that we believed the problem was more complex than adding a field or a line of code. In fact, we were pretty sure that, even if we added the field, there would still be serious problems and that her information systems department would be blamed for a failed project.

I told her that I needed two more weeks to finish my recommendations for fixing the entire problem, both programming and process. I committed to her that after she saw our report, if she felt that the work had been unnecessary, we wouldn't charge her. She gave us the two weeks, and we wound up presenting the recommendations to a group of key executives. They were so impressed with the work that our customer looked like a hero and we wound up doing millions of dollars of business with that organization.

EMBED YOUR HIGHER CALLING INTO YOUR BUSINESS STRATEGY

In order to promote a commitment to quality, it helps to embed your higher calling into your strategy. Start by defining your higher calling. Nothing bonds people together more than striving toward a noble cause or an aspirational goal. People want to have a purpose beyond earning their paychecks.

Strategic planning for most companies involves a good cross-section of the enterprise—that is, up, down, and across the organizational chart. When your higher calling is embedded into your corporate strategy, it leads to the creation of tactics for which specific action items and budgets are allocated.

Strategic plans are communicated throughout the organization to educate the workforce on the company's goals, so that each employee knows how they fit into the bigger picture. When the higher calling is a part of this process, everyone becomes engaged in understanding the mission of the company beyond its financial targets, and the higher calling is woven into the fabric of all business processes. This vision becomes as important to your firm as the rest of the business's goals.

PRINCIPLE #4

A HIGHER CALLING
Have Purpose Beyond Profits

When your business's higher calling is directly related to the quality of the service you provide, that goal inspires and provides a sense of purpose to your employees. When that happens, you have achieved the holy grail in business: purpose meeting success.

Call to Action:

» Do you know what your company's higher calling is?

» Does your company focus on customers first so that there is revenue to support your higher calling?

» Do you personally have a higher calling that can be satisfied at work?

» Is your company's higher calling supported at all levels, including the board of directors?

My Lessons Learned:

» In the early days of Healthlink, I hired nurses, doctors, pharmacists, and other healthcare professionals. I found that these people had a passion for healthcare and improving processes so that the organizations they served could do a better job of saving lives. We embraced their passion, which helped to create a purpose.

» Many of our employees could have gone elsewhere to make more money, but they stayed with us because of the strong sense of community they enjoyed and the feeling that their integrity was better served working for a company that had purpose.

» In the Catholic health systems I supported, the nuns who served on the board of directors would frequently state "no margin, no mission"—a fresh reminder that higher callings won't manifest without profits.

ACTS OF LOVE

Once, as I boarded a flight, the husband of my company's CEO stood up from his place in first class and said that his seat belonged to me. I was blown away by this kind gesture. This probably stuck with me even more than if the CEO had given up her seat!

———

We had a programmer in my office that developed ALS. As he lost his ability to type, the company bought voice recognition software for him. When that no longer worked, he stayed on advising other programmers. Near the end, the company sent him, his daughter, and a good family friend to Disney World so that the programmer could have a last vacation with his daughter. They then named an annual employee award after him.

———

My company president sent a handwritten letter via the U.S. Postal Service to my wife describing my value to the company. It was accompanied by an invitation for the two of us to go out to dinner and take in a show at the company's expense. I have in turn paid that Act of Love forward a few times with great results.

5

GOVERNANCE:
Focus on Long-Term Growth

Today, the average tenure for an American employee at any one workplace is 4.6 years.[1] Only about 1 in 10 employees spends 20 or more years with the same employer.[2] That's at least partially because "there aren't nearly as many companies that last 50 years as there used to be," says Gerald Davis, management professor at the University of Michigan's Ross School of Business and the author of Managed by the Markets. "They don't stick around the way they used to.[3]

By the latter half of the 20th century, the rise of mergers, acquisitions, reorganizations, layoffs, outsourcing, off-shoring, and bankruptcies reduced corporate stability. After remaining steady from 1930 to 1990, all but 3 of the 30 publicly traded companies that make up the Dow Jones Industrial Average have turned over since 1990.[4] Given the pace of innovation, workers didn't know whether their employers would be around in a year, much less if their jobs would still exist. The result was the erosion of both loyalty and productivity. Love and hope became diminishing resources in the workplace.

When fear becomes the driving motivator in achieving business goals, "me" before "we" can seem like the smarter option.

But work was not always a fear-based environment. Following World War II, many Americans found a job with a company, perhaps the same company that had employed their father, brother, or neighbor. It wasn't at all uncommon for employees to spend their entire careers working for one company. Kaman Aerospace in Bloomfield, Connecticut, was one such company. It wasn't unusual for employees to celebrate 35 years of service with Kaman. The founder, Charlie Kaman, knew every employee by name, as well as how many kids they had. The company took photographs of employees' families in the helicopters that their family member had helped manufacture. Each summer, the company held a picnic for their employees who were invited to bring their entire families. At the picnic, there were raffle drawings for significant prizes, such as backyard playgrounds.

People didn't leave Kaman Aerospace for better or higher-paying jobs; they stayed until they retired. They stayed because they were part of the family.

The employees offered Kaman Aerospace and companies like it a stable workforce, while the company offered its workers the promise of long-term employment, security, and a pension upon retirement. There was no expensive turnover. The employees were like rabid football fans who cheered for their home team and wouldn't dream of rooting for another one.

Some professions still enjoy the notion of company as family. Look in particular at police officers, firefighters, and those who serve in the military. There is story after story of policemen rallying to help a fellow officer's family through a health crisis, and families of servicemen and women essentially "adopting" the newborn daughter of a fallen comrade. This tells us that all is not lost. Humanity has not given up on itself. Love and hope are in each of us; it's just a matter of being a part of an environment or culture that nurtures its growth.

So, brotherhoods like firefighters and police aside, how did the rest of us end up with a generation of fear-based companies?

LEADERSHIP DISRUPTED BY MANAGEMENT SYSTEMS

As with most changes, these negative effects began with a well-intentioned new idea.

In 1954, in lockstep with increasing management hierarchies and systems of mass production, Peter Drucker wrote a book called *The Practice of Management*, which established the concept of Management by Objectives (MBO). This was intended to improve an organization's performance by establishing clearly defined goals that managers and employees agreed with and that aligned with the overall goals of the company.[5] Employees' actual performance and achievements were measured against defined objectives that they would be rewarded for achieving. This was expected to improve employee motivation and commitment, and promote better communication between employees and management.

In theory, there would have been daily feedback, and the emphasis would have been on rewards rather than on punishment. In practice, however, MBO focused too much on an unbalanced set of objectives. It transformed the manager from a leader into a bean counter. Since employees were measured against 5 to 10 goals per year, anything that wasn't explicitly written down as an objective was neglected because achieving recorded objectives was the primary factor in determining raises, promotions, and so on.

While MBO and other management systems sought to establish new baselines for more dynamic business cultures, they ended up seeding a negative shift in culture. Although employees now had a more direct say in their goals, there was a greater likelihood that they would feel pressure to set unrealistic and unachievable goals, not only for the team but also individually, which could result in cheating to achieve the goal while neglecting other important objectives.

"What gets measured gets done,"[6] the mantra of MBO, began to dominate our business schools and leadership training programs. Simple acts of kindness to employees took a backseat to micromanaged performance targets. As top-level executives became more focused on hitting quarterly financial earnings targets, customers became an irritating distraction.

None of this happened overnight. The move from love to fear emerged over decades of driving efficiencies into businesses, often in order to survive, but almost always at the expense of employees and customers.

Good people who previously felt awkward leading with fear became more comfortable doing so as they realized that, to move up the chain of command, they needed to follow corporate leadership styles like lemmings. If those same good people had been introduced to a different management style, such as following more love-based principles of leadership, they would have been far more comfortable and probably more successful.

THE SPECTER OF QUARTERLY EARNINGS

Similar to MBO, in corporate America, quarterly earnings reports have become a necessary evil. By requiring publicly traded companies to report their financial performance, these reports pressure a company's management to "hit its numbers" every three months. It narrows management's focus and overshadows other goals that should take priority. It also creates an environment in which short-term planning and decision-making eclipse long-term strategic planning. This can lead to companies that report earnings before they are actually earned or that invent data to meet projections, which runs counter to having a healthy workplace culture.

Those who watch public company operations from a distance, such as board members and investors, discount the notion that quarterly reporting impacts a company's long-term viability. Investors demand quarter-over-quarter results, CEOs are paid to achieve them, and everything flows downriver from there.

> "Being captive to quarterly earnings isn't consistent with long-term value creation. This pressure and the short-term focus of equity markets make it difficult for a public company to invest for long-term success, and tend to force company leaders to sacrifice long-term result to protect current earnings."
>
> CHARLES KOCH

However, anyone who hasn't experienced this phenomenon doesn't understand business stress. If, as a manager, you fail to hit your numbers in a quarter, you feel as if you are at the mercy of faceless, mercenary shareholders who don't really care about your company but only about the price of your stock. This is perhaps an exaggeration, but exaggeration is where fear-based cultures excel.

A recent example of the pressure caused by Wall Street's earnings expectations involves Elon Musk, the entrepreneur who founded the electric car company, Tesla, Inc. Frustrated with a system that had been in place since the 1970s, Musk had already signaled to his employees that he wanted to take his company private, in part to avoid the quarterly earnings cycle that "puts enormous pressure on Tesla to make decisions that may be right for a given quarter, but not necessarily right for the long term."[7]

The idea of eliminating quarterly earnings reports has been floated more than once to get the C-suite to focus on strategic, long-term objectives. While I was writing this book, President Donald Trump asked the Securities and Exchange Commission (SEC) to study the feasibility of allowing publicly traded companies to report earnings twice yearly instead of quarterly to ease pressure on business leaders and spur growth.[8]

The combination of the pressure to hit quarterly numbers and the excessive costs related to frequent reporting requirements underscores the need to loosen some of the restrictive regulations that contribute to a fear- and anxiety-based work culture. These contributing factors can create a vicious cycle of employee *and* company turnover, as MBO, metrics, and quantitative analysis for earnings reports lead to fear-based decisions and governance.

When short-term goals are not met, nobody talks about love, yet that's exactly what is needed. When quarterly earnings estimates are missed, the CEO needs to step up and deliver, not because employees fear failure but because they believe in their company and its mission and have a commitment to their managers and peers. This can't be accomplished when executives feel like they are operating in a fire-drill environment from quarter to quarter with the sole focus on keeping investors happy. Leaders must remain focused on long-term goals and remember that working toward these goals will manifest as much stronger financial results and success in the long run.

VOICE OF DANA

When we were just getting started at Healthlink, we were asked to work on a project for the CFO of a major healthcare system who wanted us to streamline his supply chain function. We assigned a consultant to the project who looked like a perfect fit. Bob was a supply-chain expert and told us he'd be able to do a great job.

Back in those days, Healthlink invoiced customers for a consultant's time in advance of the month's work—we didn't have a lot of money in the bank to pay consultants while we were waiting to collect receivables—so we sent an invoice to the CFO and he paid promptly even though we hadn't started the work yet.

Right off the bat, things went off track. Our supply-chain expert Bob showed up and told the CFO's assistant that he would need a parking place in the garage next to the executive office building, not in the surface lot a block away. The assistant explained that all visiting employees parked in the surface lot.

Bob insisted, and she said she'd check with the CFO.

Then Bob told her he was going to need a flip-chart stand. She brought one out for him, but he said it wasn't good enough. He showed her one he wanted in a catalog. She said the one she had available was used everywhere in their organization, even in the boardroom. "Surely," she said, "it will be good enough for you, too." But Bob was demanding. He insisted he needed a better stand.

Even as Bob was getting off on the wrong foot with his demands, it became apparent that he didn't really know how to approach *this kind of project. He stumbled right out of the gate and irritated everyone he encountered.*

Ivo and I could see we had problems, and we came up with a plan to replace Bob. We met with the client's CFO and told him we wanted to make a change to get things back on track.

Unfortunately, he told us things were beyond repair. "Even my assistant wants him out of here! We've come up with another plan and we won't be needing your help."

Clearly, we couldn't make things right by getting the project on track, so there was only one thing to do: send back the money they had already paid. That hurt. In those days, it seemed like a huge amount of money to us, but we knew we hadn't delivered value and we didn't deserve to be paid. We wrote a check to the healthcare system.

Years went by, and we began to do small projects with the same organization again, working with the information systems department this time. Eventually, we earned enough trust that we were able to do a very large and strategic project for the organization. I knew that the same CFO we had tried to work with previously would need to approve our contract, and I was afraid he would refuse. With my heart in my throat, I went to meet with him.

I explained that we were proposing to help with a really large project and wanted to understand if our failed project years before would pose a problem. He laughed out loud and said, "In my 30 years as a CFO, Healthlink is the only company that ever sent me a check without even being asked. That was amazing! Why the heck would I have a problem doing business with a company that steps up to an issue with that kind of attitude?"

Sure enough, he approved our contract, and we worked together for years in a very successful relationship—all because we had owned up to a problem and made things right. Could we have done this if we were publicly traded and beholden to short-term financial results? I doubt it.

PRINCIPLE #5
GOVERNANCE
Focus on Long-Term Growth

It is precisely because of their influence on such company wide measures as management and quarterly earnings that the impact of business culture starts in the boardroom. This idea of love-based governance ranges from a three-pronged approach to boardroom leadership to the impact of a CFO's outlook on corporate culture as a whole.

THE ROLE OF THE BOARD IN A LOVE-BASED CULTURE

Board meetings at Healthlink were not designed to be presentations but rather working sessions at which we could benefit from more experienced business leaders. This is how boards should work, but sadly most do not.

In one of our first board meetings, we had a problem that needed to be solved, and I had my first opportunity to witness the magic of this high-powered team "working the issue." This was where I learned from Compaq's Rod Canion that decisions that focused on short-term results, such as quarterly earnings, were also short-sighted. All decisions needed to be made in the best long-term interest of the company. Rod helped us create a governance team that understood the value of culture, and many of our meetings centered on how to protect and support our culture rather than on the management team merely presenting financial results. It was selfless, and therefore, it propelled the business forward.

> One of the greatest acts of courage a CEO can make is to stand up to a board in defense of the values and culture of their company, with the understanding that it could get them fired.

CEOs need to understand that boards only have a few primary functions: hiring, firing, paying the executive team, and ensuring that the company is operating legally and responsibly. They don't run the company and, indeed, are not in a position to dictate the values that you and your team embrace. If you can build your board with savvy, experienced business leaders who understand the power of culture, all the better. Unfortunately, many of today's boards are made up of financial investors who have no real business experience and only manage to the numbers. Their lack of experience with corporate cultures has, at times, cost them billions of dollars that they invested in fear-based companies that lacked transparency.

One of the greatest acts of courage a CEO can make is to stand up to a board in defense of the values and culture of their company, with the understanding that it could get them fired. I don't remember ever using the words "unconditional love" in a board meeting, but I know the feelings invoked by those words were embraced by all of our team members. Letting them down in a moment of weakness in a board meeting would have been the death of our culture. Enforcing unconditional love means enforcing love of your culture without excuses, even when it comes to the people who sign your paycheck.

Unconditional love refers to caring about the wellbeing of others without any thought for what we might get for ourselves. I was able to believe in this definition at Healthlink because I had a board of directors whom I trusted to take care of me if I took care of the company. That's rare, and I was grateful.

A board of directors should take an active role in moderating fear-based governance by thinking about the people behind the numbers and about how their actions trickle down to even the most junior employee. It's naïve to think that boards of directors are going to be overly sympathetic to a highly paid executive team whose job it is to increase the stock price of the company, but if they had any operations experience, they would comprehend the immense risk they take on by supporting a fear-based culture in which the truth of the company's performance has been hidden or violated.

THE THREE-LEGGED STOOL OF GOVERNANCE

Rod Canion was Healthlink's first chairman, and he believed that our company would be stronger with a three-legged stool in the boardroom. That is, with him as chairman, me as the CEO, and Dana as the COO. Joe Boyd later replaced Rod as chairman, but fundamentally we all believed that three legs were better than two, as in the case of those governance boards on which the CEO and chairman are the same person. After all, a stool with only two legs won't stand for long. The first two legs will always be the same: the chairman and the CEO. The third leg can be either the COO, the CFO, or some other executive who acts as what I call the "strong no. 2" to the CEO.

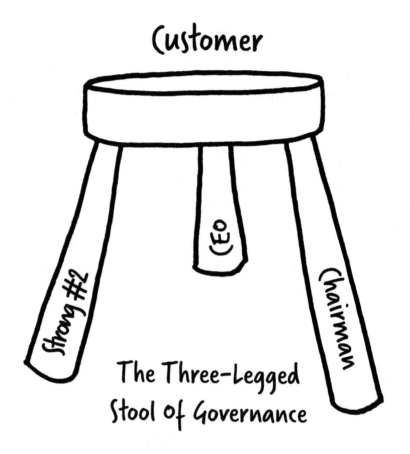

Customer

The Three-Legged
Stool of Governance

» **Option 1:** Chairman, CEO, COO - Three different people who lack trust, have unhealthy conflict and different values = BAD

» **Option 2:** Chairman/CEO, COO - Two people with trust, healthy conflict, and common values = BETTER

» **Option 3:** Chairman, CEO, COO - Three different people with trust, healthy conflict, common values = BEST

I firmly believe that Rod's three-legged stool structure is the key to a love-based boardroom. Consider Option 3 in the illustration below, compared with the two other potential means of corporate governance.

Most CEOs prefer Option 2 because of the risks inherent in Option 1, namely having to deal with unhealthy conflict while trying to steer a company towards a common vision. A CEO's desire to execute a long-term strategy while feeling the heat from a chairman to meet short-term financial goals can lead to a fear-based culture where the lack of teamwork and lack of shared values flow down into the organization.

However, a company is better protected when there are three key players all working within the framework of a common set of values. Inevitably, there will be turnover in one or more of these roles over the many years of a company's growth. By having a chairman and a COO with a common set of values, when it comes time to hire a new CEO, the board will reduce its risk of making a mistake, like hiring based on skill alone. The likelihood of a harmful lack of transparency is also minimized by this three-legged stool approach, especially if the legs work in trusting tandem.

For instance, one night I was sitting in my recliner at home when my cell phone rang. I looked down and saw that the chairman of Encore, Joe Boyd, was calling. We had recently signed an agreement to enter into a sales process for Encore, so Joe and I were speaking frequently. While Joe was the chairman of the company, I was the co-founder and majority shareholder. Dana was the CEO.

I answered his call and we exchanged a few pleasantries, but I could sense tension in his voice. He finally said, "Ivo, you're going to have to shut those two companies down right now!" He was referring to two start-ups I had announced that day, Next Wave Connect and Smart Social Media. Both Dana and I were well known in the healthcare services sector because of the success of Healthlink and Encore. Joe was concerned that the buyer of Encore would assume that the new start-ups would be "encores" to Healthlink and Encore. At that moment I made a note to self: never call a company Encore.

Joe was livid. If he had been sitting in front of me, I'm sure I would have seen his face turn as red as his bright red hair. Joe was normally a calm and collected guy, the kind of person you would want to share a beer with, but he was on a mission to do his job and get this deal closed. He was literally yelling at me, using a few profanities I didn't comprehend. Fire was blowing out of the phone.

This wasn't Joe's first rodeo in the role of chairman. I had brought him into that role while I was the CEO of Healthlink because he was a perfect fit for the position. At that stage of my career I was so deep into the details that, when it came to the company, I couldn't see the forest for the trees.

Joe saw the bigger picture and had a unique ability to know when to step back and when to swoop in and get involved. This was evident at both Healthlink and Encore when we were in the sales process for each company. Joe was instrumental in closing both deals, not because of his vision, but rather because he was capable of doing real work to get them across the finish line.

On the call, Joe reminded me that he really didn't care about any of my business ventures except the one he was closing at the moment, and we needed to be on the same team. My announcement of the two new companies could be construed as hostile to buyers, and at this stage of the transaction, there was no reason to cause an alarm to go off. I saw no reason to stop these companies from starting. I had spent months in the planning stages, and both were well capitalized. I had hired a team and was ready to roll with my next great entre-preneurial adventure.

Yet here I was, on the other end of a phone call with a man I deeply respected, a friend who had only looked out for my best interests in the past. More importantly, we shared a set of core values that allowed us to work together, frequently disagreeing but always leaving the bar arm in arm, with respect for each other.

Joe knew I was hard-headed with a strong will and that the only way to get my attention sometimes was with a big, fat, hypothetical baseball bat straight to the head. It worked. He caught my attention, and while I didn't shut the companies down, I did draw a bright line between the companies, making it clear that they would not compete and that I wouldn't aggressively advertise them until Joe finalized the Encore deal.

This would not have happened without Joe's relentless passion and the love we had for one another. Even if it doesn't sound like it, Joe's angry phone call was an Act of Love. As part of Encore's three-legged stool, he was doing what was in the best interest of the company and especially shareholders—including me.

TRANSPARENCY, TRUST, AND THE ALL-IMPORTANT FORECAST

We've spent a lot of time in this chapter talking about governance boards in and of themselves, but I'd like to change tacks and discuss their connection to the rest of a love-based company.

While love-based businesses have many financial advantages, there is one that overwhelms all others: *forecasting*. Companies live and die by their forecasts. If you are a publicly traded company, your ability to forecast earnings several quarters into the future determines today's stock price. For privately held early-stage companies, it may determine survival because making a mistake in forecasting revenues can result in a young business running out of cash.

Good forecasts only come from those at the grassroots level of your organization, the people who are closest to customers and can therefore understand their purchasing patterns and best predict when deals will close. In love-based companies, these employees want to produce an accurate forecast for their segment of the business because they know the importance it holds for the company overall.

While it's difficult for anyone to provide a forecast that doesn't meet expectations, the importance of accuracy is everything, even if a forecast is going to be a miss.

A bad forecast can reverberate throughout an entire company: you can't hire the right number of people if you don't know if you're going to have the profits to support them. The same applies to purchasing assets, growing into new markets, and expanding benefits for employees. In fear-based companies, missing your forecasts means failure, and you can be assured that stern words will be spoken if this happens.

People who work in fear-based companies don't want to deliver bad news because of the personal repercussions it might bring about. It is human nature to want to delay stress and pain rather than to experience them in the moment. In this case, however, delayed pain could result in a lack of strategic planning and inaccurate sales or expense forecasts that in turn mean an even greater amount of pain reverberating throughout the company in the long term. As Dana used to say, "Bad news doesn't get better with time."

RECTIFYING FORECAST FEAR WITH THE RIGHT TYPE OF CFO

CFOs have emerged as second to the CEO in importance to the board of directors, with a direct line between the CFO and the board for compliance issues. In fact, the most critical player in the forecasting process is the CFO. How a CFO handles forecasts is a reflection of their maturity. Are they "bean counters" or strategic professionals?

In fear-based companies, CFOs use intimidation to motivate, knowing full well that those they are asking to produce forecasts will unwittingly sabotage the company by fudging their numbers to avoid the in-the-moment wrath of the CFO and the CEO.

I've worked with CFOs who are bean counters and CFOs who are strategic professionals, and I have learned to revere those CFOs who are strategic. Having a strategic CFO is critical to a love-based culture. These people become true partners not only to the CEO and board but also to all the key executives in the company, especially those who must predict revenue and earnings. This is because instead of coming at financial projections from a reactive place of fear, they can think proactively and strategically into the long term to benefit the company as a whole.

VOICE OF DANA

Ivo and I used to argue now and then about culture. Ivo would say that our culture was so strong it would spit people out if they didn't fit in. I would argue that our culture (any culture, in fact) was incredibly fragile. If either one of us saw people behaving in a way that didn't fit our core values and then allowed the behavior to continue uncorrected, the culture would crack and eventually break. We had to be ever vigilant to protect our culture and uphold our values.

Sometimes it was hard. I remember when I began to get reports that one of our managers was not behaving in a way that was consistent with our values. I spoke with her several times, but the reports continued. She was one of our superstars in the field and had many loyal followers in the company. Having her leave the company would be a big blow. It would mean lost revenue, morale problems, and an open leadership position. But when push came to shove, what was more important: lost revenue or a crack in the culture? We chose to lose revenue in the end.

THE VITAL DIFFERENCE BETWEEN BUILDING AND BREAKING A POSITIVE CULTURE

I once sat on the board of a for-profit company. At one meeting, the chairman, a partner at a major venture capital firm, opened by asking for a closed session. He wanted to meet with board members, and board members only, while the CEO and staff waited outside the room.

He opened the closed session by stating that the CEO needed to be fired.

This took me aback. I thought highly of this CEO. He was young, smart, and, while challenged with a complicated global business, he was learning at hyper-speed and had a healthy relationship with his team.

> Breaking a culture can happen with the swift stroke of one hire, while building a culture takes decades.

I was willing to mentor and help him develop into a leader who could make this company worth a lot of money, but I never had the chance. The chairman, who owned well over 50%

of the shares in the company and could do whatever he wanted, held all the cards. The money that the chairman had put into the company gave him the controlling interest, thereby anointing him as king. (In those situations, I think they should change the title from chairman to king, but I digress.)

I've been fortunate in my career as CEO always to have had boards that were love-based. My boards featured ex-CEOs who had run businesses before and clearly understood the rough-and-tumble day-to-day processes of building a company. While some partners at venture capital firms have prior experience running a business, many join these firms straight out of Ivy League business schools, with no practical experience to speak of.

In most cases, if someone on your board unilaterally holds the power to fire the CEO, they are king. If it's your company and you're the king, congratulations. Just be careful, as you raise cash in the future, to find investors who understand your love-based culture.

Breaking a culture can happen with the swift stroke of one hire, while building a culture takes decades. I encourage you to think of this, and not your own personal gain, whenever you enter a board meeting. Put into place a strategic CFO and a three-legged governance structure, and the risk that your company will evolve to fear will be greatly reduced.

PRINCIPLE #5

GOVERNANCE
Focus on Long-Term Growth

The impact of culture on a business' financial outcomes starts at the board level. Fear-based boardroom cultures lacking in transparency have taken down a number of companies in recent years. Measuring a company's performance one quarter at a time has created a distraction to management that ultimately and negatively impacts shareholders. The role of the board in creating long-term incentives that support long-term strategies has never been more critical.

Call to Action:

» Does your board of directors contain current or ex-CEOs who have built companies and who understand the impact that a bad culture can have on stakeholders?

» Do the directors of your company focus on the long-term strategy of the company or on short-term financial results?

» How have your individual board members behaved during difficult times at past portfolio companies? Based on this information, do you feel that they will handle the heat with you and, more importantly, have your back when times are tough?

» Is there transparency at the board level of your business to the point that what's presented to the board is true to what's going on in the company?

My Lessons Learned:

» The role of the CFO is critical to a love-based culture. A love-based culture needs a CFO that can coach the company's leaders and develop trusting relationships that allow them to create accurate forecasts built from the bottom up.

» The pressure of quarterly earnings has a significant impact on long-term planning and execution. "Hitting your numbers" each quarter leads to repetitive fire drills that fuel a fear-based culture.

» Business is more than holding managers accountable for numbers. We need to return to the lost art of leadership and remember that humans respond better to carrots than to sticks.

» It's my job as the CEO to create a long-term vision for the company and build a team of executives to help me execute on that vision. My opportunity for success is greatly enhanced if I have a board of directors made up of experienced business executives and investors who share my values and can challenge and mentor me in a healthy way to build the company.

ACTS OF LOVE

I was working in Indianapolis, Indiana, when, one day, the account manager (my big boss) walked up to my cubicle and invited me to lunch. We left the building with little small talk and walked way past where folks normally went to eat. Then he turned into the downtown tennis center where the Indianapolis Clay Court Pro tournament was underway.

We proceeded to seats at center court and spent the afternoon, just the two of us, enjoying pro tennis. I would have killed for him after that. The things that made the afternoon special were (1) he somehow found out that I was a tennis fan and had played on a team in high school, (2) he invested his time with me in a personal way, and (3) we did something that had nothing to do with work. This probably cost the company $100 for the 2 seats and $20 for the beer and hot dogs, but it was the best employee recognition I'd ever experienced. I will never forget it, and I have told hundreds of people this positive story about leadership.

6

COMPENSATION:
Reward Those Who Add Value

Over the past few decades, new and innovative management systems, regulations that encourage short-term planning and decision-making, and a belief that all aspects of performance must be measured overtook the corporate environment. The resulting turn away from leading people to managing metrics has caused us to lose sight of what might have become a legacy skill: adding value to the company as a whole.

As stated in chapter 5, the role of the CFO has ascended into a position that's close to that of the CEO. CFOs ensure compliance with all regulations, obtain metrics from management systems, and conduct much more complicated financial reporting and analysis than we have seen in the distant past. The science of business has evolved.

To help managers monitor progress and success, CFOs demand metrics to measure goals and objectives. While this makes sense on paper, there's a major flaw in this thinking: much of what adds value to a company can't be measured, as much of a team member's performance is subjective. This subjective, intangible element of performance includes teamwork, collaboration, innovation, judgment, motivation, attitude, and a desire to win, just to name a few. In the world of management by objectives, if there is no metric, there is no performance, yet often what can't easily be measured is more critical and pivotal to success than what can.

Is there a benefit to gathering all these numbers and analytics? Absolutely. The better the data, the fewer surprises there will be and the better we can manage our business strategy. Data help us identify trends and stay up to date on customer demands. It helps us run a lean company without a lot of waste. Metrics to a business are like an instrument panel to a pilot: they make it easier to take off, navigate all manner of weather conditions, and land safely. I don't think anyone would want to get on an airplane with a pilot who did not understand the data on the equipment in front of him.

> ## Somehow, by driving businesses to greater efficiency, we forgot about one crucial element: HUMANS.

Similarly, running a business without considering metrics would be foolish. Yet we need to remember that the numbers are only a scorecard for long-term performance, and long-term performance is all about those superstars who rise to the occasion and make magic happen in the company. That's something that can't be measured. Somehow, by driving businesses to greater efficiency, we forgot about one crucial element: HUMANS.

Which brings me to the story of Deb.

Early in the history of Healthlink, we had a reception-ist, Deb. Deb had a dazzling smile that greeted everyone that walked through the front door. I always appreciated her cre-ating this nice first impression for employees and customers. One day, she came into my office and told me she wanted to work in the accounts payable (AP) department. These were the people who collect receipts and other expenses and made sure they are all accounted for accurately. She said, "That's where I think I can help the most."

As she was talking, I thought, "Are you kidding me? Why would anybody want to do that job?" but she had been a good, loyal employee. As soon as a position opened up, she moved over.

A year or so later, I walked into my office, and there she was again. She said, "I want to work in the IT department." Ap-parently she had been reading networking books in her spare time and was planning on taking some classes on the subject. Receptionist to AP to IT was not a normal progression, but again, she had done a good job. We preferred to promote from within, so why not?

As the company grew, Deb kept taking classes and used her knowledge to make our IT infrastructure better, until she eventually landed the role of chief information officer. Quite an accomplishment, considering she had started as a temp re-ceptionist. During this time I had hired a CFO, John, who had a much harder edge to him than his predecessors. I had ratio-nalized him as fitting in based on my impression that a CFO needed to be tough and instill discipline into an organization. I should also mention that John was Deb's boss.

John had a lot of opinions on how people should lead and how departments should be run. He didn't listen; he talked. He expected all of his managers to do things his way and not push back. In other words, he was a fear-based leader. Deb, on the other hand, had grown with the company and fully embraced a team culture in which every voice is heard. She looked out for the company first and her own interests second. She had also worked with leaders who expected her to speak out and share her opinions. Deb did not like John, and John did not like Deb. I had many a counseling session with them, trying to help them move closer to center. It didn't work.

One day, without even a knock, my door burst open. Deb stormed in, all 5 feet and 100 pounds of her, declaring, "You have to fire John!" I politely told her I was on a call and that we'd chat when I was done, so she marched out of my office, shutting the door on her way.

Two minutes later my door burst open again. This time it was John, not noticing I was on a call, who yelled, "I'm going to fire Deb!" I politely told him I was on a call and would get back to him shortly.

After finishing my call, I learned that John had told Deb that if she didn't start doing what she was told without questioning him, he was going to fire her. She pushed back, which started an argument. The argument had devolved into a screaming match that ended with him cornering her and pointing his finger in her face.

I fired John the next day, and once I got a deeper understanding of the problems he had created for all of his other managers, I developed an even greater appreciation for Deb. She was the one manager who had put her foot down and taken the risk of challenging me for hiring someone who was destructive to the company. This woman was so protective of our culture that she had put her own job on the line to save it.

BEING A TEAM PLAYER MEANS MORE THAN HITTING YOUR INDIVIDUAL GOALS

What value did Deb add to the company? Her actions would not have shown up on any metrics that could have been linked to her individual performance. On performance reviews, she was measured on customer satisfaction scores, computer availability and response time, etc. There was no metric for the role she took in protecting the company's culture, yet as I reflect back on her actions, what she did added tremendous value to Healthlink. Had she not forced me to open my eyes to John's destructive behavior, we may not have been as successful. I suspect that eventually I would have realized that John just didn't fit in, but it's hard to imagine the damage he might have done in the meantime.

To repair the damage that's been done by fear-based, metric-reactive governance like John's, we must restore trust with and within our teams. One way to do this is to create love-based compensation processes and procedures.

Deb deserved credit for her actions. To only pay her based on her competency in managing IT infrastructure and not consider her role in making our company a much better place for everybody to work would be shortsighted. Her compensation ultimately needed to be linked to the overall value she brought to the company, not solely on her individual performance metrics, so what she did, along with her other performance goals, all counted toward how she should be compensated.

You may find that love-based compensation is an uphill battle. Young employees today know nothing other than the current atmosphere in which it is normal, and even encouraged, to change jobs 4 or more times before they turn 30. Businesses appear and disappear so quickly that today's cutting-edge career is tomorrow's obsolete job. These young employees' perceived self-value is only as high as their current salary, so they're constantly on the lookout for the next step toward growth and relevancy. In their experience, what else is there? This is all in contrast with an emerging workforce that cares more about intangibles, such as values and higher callings, than money. So, how can we compensate them from a place of love?

PRINCIPLE #6
COMPENSATION
Reward Those Who Add Value

Love-based compensation programs should focus not just on easily quantifiable end results, but also (and especially) on making measurable the subjective elements of an employee's job performance that lead to their individual and team-based success. It should be noted that, for service-based companies, teamwork may be of more significance than individual success, while individual success may be a more helpful subjective metric category for commodities-based businesses.

VOICE OF DANA

Before joining Healthlink, I had always thought of myself as a team player. It was on our very first project at Healthlink, though, that I totally bought into the power of teamwork. Working with our first client, we were asked to complete a task that I had perfected over hundreds of other client projects. As a result, I had a very detailed multi-page project plan that had been tested and improved over the years, and I knew exactly what needed to be done.

But my colleague Jeff said, "Not so fast!" He told me we'd have better results if we formed a team that brought together all of our key stakeholders and let them develop the plan. I was skeptical—my plan was proven to work!—but I agreed to let Jeff, our teamwork guru, go through the exercise. In the back of my mind, I was thinking, I'll let them take a stab at it, then I'll whip out my plan and show them what really needs to be done!

So, we formed the team and let them work together in a three-hour session. When they were done, I compared my plan, honed over years of hard work, to theirs. What I discovered blew me away. This team of novices had managed to think of almost every line item in my detailed plan! And here's what really made the difference: the people who developed the plan were the same people we needed on board as we executed the plan. Because they had developed it, they understood what needed to be done, and they owned it because they had come up with it together. If I had plopped down my very smart plan, we would have had a hard time putting it into action because our team would have felt that the brass was ordering them around.

WOW! A three-hour investment of time had saved us months of delays and problems. In one short afternoon, I became a believer in the power of teamwork.

Since then, I've worked with some incredible teams, but that very first team I worked with at Healthlink stands out as the best I've ever been part of:

> Jeff Pferd came to us from a geology background. He didn't know anything about healthcare, but he more than made

up for that with his knowledge of how to form successful teams. Jeff taught us how to engage stakeholders, how to use team tools and techniques, and how to get work done in a fun, productive way.

Karen Knecht was our resident clinical expert. Karen knew the ins and outs of healthcare, and she had mastered the art of seeing where healthcare was headed. She made sure we kept the patient at the heart of everything we did.

Dave Niemeyer was our technical guru, but he also brought to the table an uncanny ability to see things in black and white, to cut through the gray areas and get to the heart of any issue. With one quick, insightful comment, Dave could snap us all out of indecision and get us moving in the right direction.

Each of these people brought their special knowledge and expertise to the table, but they also had complementary personalities that let all of us perform at our very best.

This team was instrumental in getting Healthlink off the ground and forming the very first concepts of what our company would be. We all felt privileged to be able to create a company from scratch and to get to do it right. Over beer, we talked about how we wanted our company to feel, how we wanted to treat our customers, and how we wanted to win, win, win. Together in the car one day, we brainstormed our first draft of what would become Healthlink's core values. We developed our first strategic plan and created the outline of what became our first employee handbook. Piece by piece, we were laying the foundation for what would become Healthlink's corporate culture.

In those initial discussions, we never used the word love, but we described what I've come to know about love-based culture, us-

ing words like respect, trust, transparency, honesty, and fun. We didn't know we were helping to build a love-based culture, but we were.

As Healthlink grew, we all went on to play different roles, but each of these core team members continued to lead by example when it came to our culture. There's no way that Ivo and I could have created the culture we had at Healthlink by ourselves. When it comes to culture, as with so many other things, it takes a team to get it right.

ASSIGNING A VALUE TO SUBJECTIVE ASPECTS OF EMPLOYEE PERFORMANCE

Occasionally at Healthlink, we would have a troubled project that required us to pull in whomever was necessary to avoid losing a client. Sometimes the person with the best skills and experience to fix the problem was working full-time on other projects, which meant they could only help at night and on weekends. Without uttering a word of complaint, these superstars would rise to the occasion and spend whatever time they had to help their fellow employees. It wasn't their project, they had no metric tied to making the troubled project successful, but they knew that we valued and needed their skills. They respected the work that the company did. As a result, they didn't hesitate to be a team player because their actions were essential to the company's overall success.

How do you measure the value of an individual like this? How do you measure the value of the employee who evaluates new hires for their fit within a company's culture? How do you measure the performance of the subject-matter expert whose value can't be represented on a spreadsheet? These people were vital parts of our team and our process. As a result, we had to develop our own ways of evaluating and valuing people's contributions to Healthlink.

Ultimately, we developed a peer-reviewed ranking system that I'll explain later in the chapter. For now, it should be stated that a ranking process only works in a love-based culture in which there is trust and in which employees believe their managers are honestly looking out for their best interests. It does not work in fear-based cultures where the employee worries that their manager is using compensation to gain political advantage and loyalty.

Basing compensation on subjective measures of performance would never work in a fear-based company because there is little trust between employees and management. In this case, employees might assume they'd be subject to the politics of the company in which rankings are based on friendships, favoritism, or other non-value considerations, or that managers would rig the system to make sure their favorites earn the most points. Why, then, would an employee contribute to the success of someone else's project when their efforts wouldn't even be acknowledged? They may help their colleagues because it's what they're told to do, but it won't be because they trust that they'll be appreciated for going above and beyond their defined role.

THE SLIPPERY SLOPE OF METRICS-BASED COMPENSATION

At the highest levels of large, publicly traded companies, there are clear metrics that define success. That's not the case as you move down the organizational chart. In these large companies, it is easy to hold executives of business units accountable for financial performance; it becomes more difficult when you rely on teams to drive success and need team members to be flexible in the roles that they play. As a result, a metric-driven accountability program can fly in the face of what's ultimately required to succeed and may in fact drive behaviors that are contrary to what will add value to the company.

It seems illogical to argue against using individual accountability goals as compensation markers, but when employees perform their jobs in a love-based culture, look out for the best interests of the company, and trust that their bosses will notice what they've done, you have an atmosphere in which everyone has the incentive to move the puck in the same direction and win.

> Basing compensation on subjective measures of performance would never work in a fear-based company because there is little trust between employees and management.

While on the surface this statement may be easy to agree with, the fact is that it also requires acceptance of subjectivity (i.e., opinions with little hard, supporting data) to determine performance. Subjective opinions on performance require trust.

One of the biggest subjective contributions I look at is WINNING. As a sports fan, I am in awe of athletes who always find a way to win. They may not have dramatically better stats than their teammates, but when the game is on the line, they know how to pull off the win. Their ability to win can't be measured like a vertical jump, their speed, or the weight they can bench-press. There is no way to quantify the intangibles that make sports legends. When others might crack under extreme pressure, these athletes dig deep and find the inner resources they need to get the job done. They trust in themselves, in their coaches, and in their teammates. They believe they can do it, so it gets done.

The same is true for business. There are team members who know how to win. They aren't smarter or better looking than anyone else. They aren't necessarily the ones who impress you in meetings or always say the right thing to the boss, but when everything is on the line, they help the team win.

IMPLEMENTING LOVE-BASED COMPENSATION IN YOUR COMPANY

The challenge with acknowledging that performance measurement is subjective rather than metrics-driven is how to tie it to compensation. Because compensation is one of the single biggest extrinsic motivators for employees, creating a system that rewards their value to the company regardless of their success in achieving individual performance goals can be a challenge. Even people who work for love-based cultures and want to serve the greater good are not so Pollyannaish that they don't also want to be paid. Money is, and will continue to be, a scorecard.

To avoid making performance measurement wishy-washy, when evaluating the immeasurable activities that support a company's success, first consider:

» Does the employee have a good attitude?

» Do they contribute substantially to the higher calling of the organization?

» Do customers consider them indispensable?

» Are they capable of guiding and mentoring subordinates?

» Do they demonstrate the company's core values in everything they do?

» Do you win deals specifically because of the value this employee brings to a client?

» Do they call "BS" when they see the company moving away from core values?

Next, find a way to make these subjective questions measurable.

RANKING TEAM MEMBERS BASED ON VALUE

At Healthlink, we solved the problem of compensation for subjective criteria by using a peer-reviewed ranking system based on the value people added to the company rather than on individual performance goals. Our managers would meet with their peers and have an in-depth discussion about team members' accomplishments and about the value those team members brought to the company. Managers would ask each other hard questions to determine if an individual added more or less value than other ranked employees.

Though each team member had individual performance goals that factored into their ranking, other subjective factors affecting the company also came into play. The fact is that the priorities of any employee can change every month, sometimes every week, as business challenges change and markets shift. While an employee may have goals for their specific job, no performance evaluation can fully anticipate an impending crisis, the need for specialized hiring, surprise resignations, unexpected acquisitions, or any of the thousands of things that can happen during a business year.

After a thorough discussion of both objective and subjective contributions, everyone on the team was ranked according to the value they added to the company. Those at the top of the ranked list were paid the most and received bonuses, while those at the bottom were put on a plan to improve or were separated from the company.

Adding overall value to the company has no metric because it is a subjective measurement of how well an employee illustrates the core values of the company while doing whatever it takes to help make the company successful, often performing tasks that were not imagined when the individual's performance plan was created.

This can result in a middle-of-the-organizational-chart employee's contributions being ranked as highly as those individuals in management. How could that be? Perhaps they developed a breakthrough product that dramatically enhanced the value of the company. Perhaps they were subject-matter experts whose credibility took a deal across the finish line. They may have volunteered to develop methodologies for new services on their own time. Regardless of where they were on the organizational chart, their contribution was weighed and valued equally.

This ranking system supported a love-based culture because those who ranked at the top were people who worked well in a team environment, raised everyone else up with their leadership, demonstrated the company's core values, and were able to accomplish great things due to their ability to take advantage of the resources the company had to offer. And yes, they also hit their individual targets as long as those targets were relevant to improving the overall value of the company.

VOICE OF DANA

One of the first times I understood the difference between "value to the organization" and "position in the org chart" was early in my career at IBM. As a systems engineer, part of my job was to manage the implementation of large, expensive mainframe computers in petrochemical companies. Back then, these systems rented for huge amounts of money, and if there was a delay in getting the system operational, IBM lost a lot of money.

One day, I found myself thinking about who the most significant contributors were in the implementation process. Of course, the salesman who sold the system got a lot of credit for closing the deal, but there were other folks who were important to a successful install and a happy client. One was a guy named Rick.

Rick sat in a little cube and never met the customer. I suspect that he was pretty low on the organizational chart. Rick was responsible for making sure all the cables and connectors showed up when the mainframe arrived. If he made a mistake, we could wind up waiting a month or two for some special cable to make its way from Japan. All the while, the customer would become more and more frustrated and IBM would lose revenue.

Rick's attention to detail made all the difference between a successful implementation and a poor one. Rick was highly valuable, and he made both the customer and me successful. The management at IBM realized how pivotal his role was to the company's overall success, which was reflected in Rick's compensation.

LOVE-BASED APPRAISALS

While compensation was based on rankings, we also performed appraisals twice annually to ensure that the employees' ranking and their perception of their performance were aligned.

I had given thousands of performance appraisals in my career, but once I recognized that there could be many definitions of success, I changed my methodology so that every person was more than the sum of their quantifiable actions.

In a love-based culture, there must be recognition that not all performance issues can be quantified and totted up to 100%. With this in mind, I came up with a few categories in which performance could be measured. I gave those categories a total weight of 50%. I then created a second category called WIN, which addressed the intangibles discussed above. The total of the items in the WIN category also received a weight of 50%. This new methodology gave me a chance to talk about teamwork, innovation, sound judgment, and other factors with an employee who may have excelled in those areas but had never been given credit for those efforts.

HYBRID COMPENSATION PROGRAMS

It's critical to understand that this ranking process is not the only way to handle compensation in a love-based company. Any compensation program that acknowledges an employee's added value to the company first and individual performance second can work.

Remember that I ran a professional services firm in which teamwork enhanced our probability of closing deals. Other businesses for which teamwork is less important, especially those that sell products, may well find success with individual incentives.

Since many companies today lack clean lines between providing strategic services (which involve a complex sales process and multiple stakeholders to close a deal) and selling products (which could be sold by a single individual whose performance could be motivated by a commission program), hybrid compensation programs that focus on both individual and team success are needed. This same concept can apply in any environment where incentives need to be based on individual versus team performance.

THE IMPACT OF PERFORMANCE-BASED COMPENSATION ON COMPANY CULTURE

Compensation management gone wrong can have one of the most destructive impacts on the culture of a company. Getting it right is essential to creating a healthy, love-based culture.

Our goal at Healthlink was to create management systems that gave our best players room to run, room to innovate, and an opportunity to take risks outside of their box of performance metrics. We needed to create an environment in which they could win and be recognized for their heroics.

In a love-based culture, rewards and recognition should go to those who help make the overall company successful. Doing anything less than that would mean that we didn't believe in the value of the team. The employee who dropped everything to help a colleague may have contributed more to the company than if they had stayed solely focused on their own assigned task.

I've been through numerous experiences where new sales leaders want to implement the sales process from their previous company along with some kind of incentive compensation program just for the sales department. Changing that one process would have a collateral impact on compensation for those who support sales, as well as for account managers of large clients who may be responsible for add-on business and training programs outside of sales. Businesses are much like dominos lined up in long, complex patterns: when one aspect is impacted, they all are eventually impacted.

Bottom Line: Love-based cultures require an all-in attitude in which every aspect of the business incorporates the concepts of teamwork, trust, and, you guessed it, love. A company's compensation programs, regardless of department, should all be linked in support of the culture. They need to be aligned with the singular focus of adding long-term value to the entire company.

PRINCIPLE #6

COMPENSATION
Reward Those Who Add Value

Employees who add the greatest overall value to the company need to be paid accordingly, regardless of what their individual performance metrics indicate. This requires employees to trust their managers' knowledge of their contribution. Judging performance is more subjective than objective, so that metrics become just one of many contributions into compensation decisions.

Call to Action:

» Do you trust your manager to make decisions on your salary increases and bonuses based on their knowledge of the contribution(s) you've made to the company?

» Do those people whose contributions impact the company have the ability to lift the team to higher levels? Do they have an opportunity to make more money based on these team-oriented contributions?

» Do you think that your compensation should be impacted by how well the company performed, regardless of your individual performance?

My Lessons Learned:

» Compensation drives behavior. A compensation plan that rewards employees for contributing to the overall value of the company requires leaders who recognize the people who are raising the bar for their entire team, rather than those who expect individual recognition.

» Performance appraisals need to be based more on a manager's subjective opinion of an employee's performance than on metrics. This requires trust between the manager and employee that is only found in love-based cultures.

» A way of measuring the value that an employee brings to the organization is to rank them relative to their peers, where the criteria is based on how a person helped the overall company achieve its goals. The people at the top represent those who added the most value, and those at the bottom are evaluated as to whether they should stay with the company. I always believed that low-ranked employees were preventing me from hiring superstars.

ACTS OF LOVE

Like Secret Santa, my office had a "secret kindness" activity for which everyone submitted a form that listed their favorite things. Then, for two months out of the year, you got your assigned person one of their favorite things each week. There was a box in the boss' office we put our items in, and every Friday, she handed the items out. This was a small Act of Love, but it made work a nicer place.

———

For a project, I was the lone rookie on what I discovered was an all-star team of seasoned professionals. Our consulting firm's CEO was on site to make herself available and help in any way. I watched in awe as she went seamlessly from meeting with the key client stakeholders to showing concern for individual consultants.

As the week came to a close and I was boarding the plane that would get me home around midnight, I passed her in first class. To my utter bewilderment, she recognized me, called me by name, and literally jumped out into the aisle to block my path. At the same time, she traded her boarding pass for mine, grabbed her luggage from the overhead compartment, and offered me her first-class seat. We exchanged insistences briefly until she made it very clear to me this was not an offer, and explained that she never lets any of her employees sit behind her on a plane.

I sat in disbelief the whole flight home, contemplating how I now wanted to make it to a place someday where I could show her a return on her investment in me.

7

WINNING:
Feel the Buzz of Success

Back in the caveman days, fear saved our lives. We escaped from predators, hunted food, ran from animals with huge teeth, and protected our families. The amygdala, an almond-shaped structure in the brain, evolved with the specific role of alerting us to such threats. Its intention was to alert us to danger so that we could react to assure our physical protection. It was not meant to keep the body in a state of constant alert.

We no longer need to lose sleep over the threat of saber-toothed cats, but today, though we live in one of the most peaceful times in Earth's history, stress is at an all-time high. This chronic stress is largely a byproduct of our inability to use fear to our advantage. We've become preoccupied by the notion that we must overcome or ignore our fear to be happy, which in turn stresses us out even more.

This information may seem counterintuitive, given my earlier explanations of love-based cultures being good and fear-based cultures being bad. However, this chapter will explain the nuances of beneficial, "acute" fear as well as what tough love can look like. These nuanced subcategories can help you create and maintain a feeling of "winning" and achievement in your workplace.

WHEN IS FEAR GOOD?

Fear can be good when it forces us to prepare and plan. Fear of failing pushes us to dive deeper into understanding risk and preparing for worst-case scenarios. Through fear, we can develop a heightened awareness of the business environment we're in, thus weighing each of our decisions carefully against the realistic implications of success or failure.

When we are feeling the pressure of intense competition and must move with great dexterity and speed, the fear of losing propels us to action. Fear is a motivator especially when there is a crisis. Fear becomes bad when it is chronic and when we do not use it to our strategic advantage, instead reacting to crisis and potential failure with negative emotions like panic and paralysis, or by lashing out in anger.

It can be easy to paint failure as the worst possible outcome, but remember, without failure, there is also little learning or growth. Failure is inevitable, and anyone with any experience in business will agree that they learned more from spilling blood and breaking bones than from all their happy victories. Those who are authentic and transparent leaders share their lessons learned from failure so that others can learn from them.

With this in mind, have a healthy, motivating fear of failure, but don't let it control you or turn your stomach in knots. There is a percentage of likelihood that you will fail at some point in your career, but if you use fear to carefully plan for the contingency of failure, you can hopefully make it less painful than if you had charged blindly ahead, not even considering failure as an option.

A STRATEGIC APPROACH TO FEAR

The Art of War, written by Sun Tzu, a Chinese general and military strategist, is as applicable today as it was when he wrote it in the late sixth century BC. The book is composed of 13 chapters, and each chapter focuses on a different aspect of war. Below are some of Sun Tzu's key points:

> "He will win who knows when to fight and when not to fight."

> "He will win who knows how to handle both superior and inferior forces."

> "He will win whose army is animated by the same spirit throughout all its ranks."

> "He will win who, himself prepared, waits to take the enemy unprepared."

> "He will win who has military capacity and is not interfered with by the sovereign." [1]

In Sun Tzu's world, fear of failure was replaced by impeccable strategy and tactical planning. We can use this lesson today: any time spent worrying about failing is time not spent preparing for the battles we face day to day while building and growing our businesses.

I believe that Sun Tzu's army embraced a love-based culture. They had a higher calling, a common set of values, and relied on each other to win. Note his advice to leadership:

> "When the common soldiers are too strong and their officers too weak, the result is insubordination. When the officers are too strong and the common soldiers too weak, the result is collapse."

"When the higher officers are angry and insubordinate, and on meeting the enemy give battle on their own account from a feeling of resentment, before the commander-in-chief can tell whether or not he is in a position to fight, the result is ruin."[2]

As I was reading *The Art of War*, I kept thinking, "Man, I would not want to be competing with this dude!" For me, Sun Tzu represents the kind of competitor who uses his market intelligence to determine attack strategy. He chose strong leadership that was best aligned to his battle strategy and trained soldiers who operated as a team respectful of their leadership. Every war was different based on the many factors that it brought to bear, but if from all his data Sun Tzu could avoid fighting and win through some other means, he took that path.

In other words, Sun Tzu made the conversion of fear of failure into strategic preparation an act of love for his troops. This mental shift leads to our seventh principle, a winning atmosphere in the workplace.

PRINCIPLE #7

WINNING
Feel the Buzz of Success

There's a magical feeling when you work for a love-based company that's firing on all cylinders. When customers and employees enjoy the effects of discipline, superior quality of products and services, happiness, and a sense of purpose, the result creates a "buzz" in and around the company that is contagious. It should be emphasized here that the focus of winning is on the company as a whole, as well as on your customers. Unfortunately, sometimes, it is necessary to maintain that sense of winning through tough love for individual employees.

WHEN IS TOUGH LOVE NECESSARY?

Starting, running, and growing a business from the ground up is hard work, and doing so within a love-based culture might suggest that the business has easier or softer expectations for its employees. This couldn't be further from the truth. There are no participation trophies in business. Business is hard and you have to have a certain level of savvy toughness to survive.

> "Know your opponent and you will never lose; know yourself and you will always win."
>
> SUN TZU, *THE ART OF WAR*

It is critical to keep an external perspective on your company in which customers come first. Otherwise, drinking too much of your own love-infused Kool-Aid can make you just one more example of how 9 out of 10 businesses fail. It's important to understand that while love-based cultures possess strong attributes that look out for the greater good of the company rather than any single individual, they also strive to win in competitive situations and to provide outstanding service to customers. When the bar is set high, some employees will not be able to rise to that level.

Under those circumstances, our most compassionate acts in business are also our most difficult. My job as CEO of Healthlink sometimes involved showing tough love by separating people from the company who didn't perform well or just didn't fit into our love-based culture. If you don't have tough conversations with employees who don't fit within your company, the situation can turn into a lose-lose for everybody. Relying on teams in love-based cultures makes people who don't fit with the culture stand out. Your employees should want to be a part of a successful team that adds value to the company. Keeping dead weight around makes it harder for them to succeed.

> There are no participation trophies in business. Business is hard and you have to have a certain level of savvy toughness to survive.

VOICE OF DANA

For me, tough love was always about doing what was right: right for the customer, right for the employee, and right for the company. One of the toughest situations I faced was when I discovered that a manager had committed a serious violation of sound business practices.

John had been working overseas, so I spoke with him first by phone on a Friday evening. He told me there had been an urgent situation and that he dealt with it in a way that he thought was in the customer's best interest. Unfortunately, his solution was a severe breach of our business practices. I decided that we needed to discuss this face to face, and I told him to get on a plane and meet me in my office first thing Monday morning.

John asked if he was going to be fired. I answered honestly: "I'm not sure what I'm going to do. Come in and let's talk." I know that I didn't sleep well that weekend, and I'm sure that John didn't either.

Bright and early Monday morning, John was in my office. As we talked, it became clear that what he had done was very wrong, but his intention had come from the right place. John had acted for the benefit of the customer, not for himself. During our conversation, I decided that John needed a refresher on sound business practices and closer supervision.

John went on to be highly successful at Healthlink. From that day on, he always adhered to sound business practices. I'm sure he never forgot that trip across the ocean!

Self-awareness becomes crucial because you need to know that you are walking the walk of your love-based culture. If you are truly creating a love-based culture and someone doesn't fit within it, then it is usually because they are operating from a place of fear or another negative emotion that could compromise the company's winning culture. They either recognize this on their own and leave or get spit out like watermelon seeds.

That said, there is a right and a wrong attitude to have in the process of dealing with people who can't rise to the occasion. They aren't bad people just because they don't fit, and they deserve to be treated with the same amount of respect as any other employee in the organization.

Love-based cultures don't require you to give an employee every chance to succeed, but it also isn't necessary to create a "three strikes and you're out" system. In your heart, you know when someone needs to move on. Often you know and everybody around this person knows that they aren't a good fit, but some people lack awareness of their own situation. There have been times, in the weeks and months before a separation, that my communication skills toward poor-fit employees could have been better, but it was still necessary to make the separation.

Once you know that an employee is no longer a good fit, act on that knowledge. People who don't fit into a love-based culture have a negative impact upon it. How you respond here is critical.

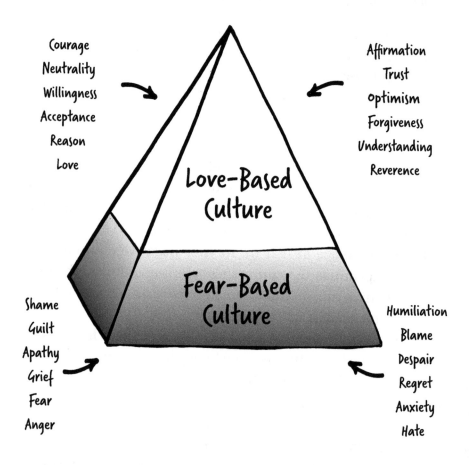

LOVE, FEAR, AND THE EMOTIONS THAT CREATE THEM

The pyramid on the previous page depicts a loose ranking of emotions. (Please note: this is my own ranking; it has no scientific basis.) The emotions listed around the pyramid lead to either fear or love, which then lead to other fear- or love-based emotions, and so on. Fear-based emotion can be a vicious cycle. Because of the neural pathways we wear into our brains in order to form habits, it can be tough to get out of these cycles once we get them going.

I wish I could say that I ran companies exclusively in the emotional states at the top of the pyramid, but sadly I did not. In the heat of competition, it was tempting for me to drop into the lower emotions. Sometimes, as stated above, these emotions generate the fear necessary for action in a crisis. However, continuing to manage with fear and anger will, in the long term, have the opposite effect.

When low-level emotions creep into our behavior, it is easy for them to create a domino effect. For example, there was a woman who helped me with this book. I needed information on obtaining releases for use of some quotes, so I emailed her with a few questions. I didn't get a response within a few days, so I sent a follow-up email. Again, there was no response.

At this point in the book-writing process, I was waking up every morning living and breathing the contents of this book—which I later realized was not a particularly healthy approach, I might add. When I still received no response, I drafted a firmer email demanding one. The more I wrote, the angrier I got, until finally, in the last line of my email, I wrote, "And if you can't find the time to get this done, I'll use my own people."

I copied the woman's boss on the email. 'That ought to get a response,' I thought. I slammed my finger onto the ENTER key and sent the email.

As soon as I sent it, I realized my mistake. Here I was, writing a book about love at work, and in the process, I had used a technique to create fear. To make matters worse, anger begets anger. I got an immediate series of zinger emails from the woman's boss. What bothered me wasn't the boss' zingers but the fact that I had been rude to her employee, someone who was trying to help me and likely had a good reason for not responding promptly. I apologized to the woman and we moved on, but the situation gave me a fresh reminder of how easy it can be to descend into anger and lash out.

We all need to understand that negative emotional behavior breeds more negative emotional behavior and keeps us firmly in the red zone of the Love/Fear Continuum. I don't know if my email created an emotion of anger, fear, guilt, or shame in the woman who was helping me or in her boss, but I can guarantee that it didn't generate feelings of love, trust, compassion, or gratitude.

How could I have handled this problem differently? I should have sent the woman a note asking for a phone call that day so I could communicate with her in real time about the impact her lack of responsiveness had on my frustration and productivity, all in an authentic and loving way.

In the distant past, I had been the master of sending out these low-level emails without thinking of the impact they might have on the recipient. Anger converts to fear and moves at the speed of light across fiber-optic lines. You can't reverse the transaction, but you can be aware of your behavior and its likely impact. As a result, you can raise your consciousness as you interact with employees in the future.

This act of consciousness-raising also gives you a chance to understand the nature of the problem—in this case why the woman hadn't responded to me. She and I are back on good terms now. I think her boss also bounced back after descending into her own low-level emotions, but I will need to address that eventually as well. It's not hard to know when you are operating in the mode of low-level emotions: you can feel it when you send out rude, condescending, and threatening emails, however professional your tone may be.

Before sending a similar message, ask yourself: Are you sending an email that will invoke fear, guilt, or shame in the reader? Or are you communicating that you are available to help, that the person you are writing to is a key part of your team, and that, while this particular effort may not have been successful, many in the future will succeed?

Highly motivated people will put themselves into the penalty box after an incident in which you offer your help and express feelings of teamwork because that's how they're wired. Those same people will also rise to the occasion and hit a grand slam the next time they are at bat. Your job is not to reinforce the negative emotions of guilt and shame that the recipient already feels, but to raise them up so they can get back into the upper-level emotions in which they refuse to let anything get in the way of their happiness and success.

THE DISTRESSING EFFECTS OF CHRONIC FEAR

I find it ironic that, while most businesses provide healthcare coverage to their employees, their fear-based cultures are responsible for many of the healthcare issues and associated costs we have today.

In 2015, Harvard and Stanford Business Schools published a working paper that evaluated 10 common job stressors.[3]

These ranged from spending long hours at work, which correlates with an increase in occupation-related injuries; to a lack of health insurance; to ongoing concerns about job security. Researchers then evaluated whether these stressors affected mortality. The findings were stunning, but perhaps they shouldn't have been.

Stress-related illnesses cost an estimated $180 billion per year in healthcare expenses.[4] Serious stress-related illnesses, such as cardiovascular disease and hypertension, kill about 120,000 people each year. According to the study's authors, this makes "work-related stressors and the maladies they cause more deadly than diabetes, Alzheimer's, or influenza."[5] The study also found that "highly demanding jobs raised the odds of a physician-diagnosed illness by 35%."[6] Clearly, stress is killing us!

According to the American Institute of Stress—yes, there is such an organization!—job stress carries an even greater price tag for the U.S. when other factors are considered: accidents; absenteeism; employee turnover; diminished productivity; workers' compensation awards; and direct medical, legal, and insurance costs. These amount to an estimated over $300 billion per year.[7]

Other studies found that the situation is getting worse, not better. A poll conducted jointly by the Harvard T. H. Chan School of Public Health, National Public Radio, and the Robert Wood Johnson Foundation found that "one in five working adults (20 percent) say they have experienced a great deal of stress at work in the past 12 months." The types of stress cited included working 50 or more hours per week, caring for a sick family member, or working in what they described as a "dangerous job."[8]

Studies have shown that "people who don't have–and prioritize–loving relationships are far more at risk for heart disease, gastrointestinal issues, mental health disorders, substance abuse problems, and more."[9] This is, of course, something you've heard many times throughout your life, but what does it mean in terms of business?

We spend most of our waking hours at work. Therefore, the workplace should be a sanctuary of love and peace, not of fear. It should be a place where love grows and flourishes rather than a place one dreads coming to. Where love is present, employees are motivated to try harder and succeed. Where fear exists, there is hesitation, silence, and even withholding of valuable information.

VOICE OF DANA

I remember a board meeting at which we were asked to list the challenges faced by the company. Near the top of the list was the concern that our employees were going to burn out.

Rod Canion, who was the chairman of our board at the time, asked why we were concerned about burnout. I explained that people were working long hours. Rod wisely told us that long hours and hard work don't lead to burnout; burnout happens when that first inkling enters your mind that you won't be successful. A poorly handled fear of failure is more likely to lead to burning out than working really hard.

CAN THERE BE GOOD STRESS?

As Sun Tzu's observations suggest, stress can be good if it is acute, not chronic, and if we respond to it proactively and strategically. However, *distress* is bad. Consider that, when we physically exercise, we stress our bodies for their overall improvement; it is when we overdo it (i.e., cause distress) that we injure ourselves.

With this in mind, it's impossible to eliminate stress from even a love-based company. Human behavior dictates that highly motivated people who are used to success will feel stressed when they stare into the jaws of possible defeat, but they use this stress to their growth and benefit. Fear of failure is one of the most pervasive emotions in life, regardless of the level of teamwork, support, and compassion you feel around you.

In a love-based company, fear is primarily self-induced and driven by a strong desire not to disappoint those who are dependent upon you to succeed. Letting your teammates, boss, or even family members down can feel like a crushing blow to people who have a history of success.

I label the fear experienced in fear-based companies as "chronic" fear because it is so deeply embedded in management styles and supporting systems that it never goes away. It's pervasive and integrated into the fabric of the company. You feel it from the moment you enter the front door until you leave at the end of the day, and then experience it again the following day. You may even experience it on the weekends or in the late evenings, as you prepare to go to work again the following morning.

As mentioned earlier, acute fear can be your friend when needed in a crisis; it comes and goes. "Chronic" fear creates unhealthy stress and is a key cause of many physical and mental health issues today.

A company that leans toward love on the Love/Fear Continuum will exhibit many of the same symptoms of fear-based companies when it is in survival mode. The difference, however, is that this fear is not "chronic." The love-based business will rely on the strength of teams to pull itself out of the ditch, solve the crisis at hand, or even downsize the company before dialing back toward love.

> In a love-based company, fear is primarily self-induced and driven by a strong desire not to disappoint those who are dependent upon you to succeed.

TRANSPARENCY AND FORGIVENESS TO COMBAT CHRONIC STRESS AND FEAR

I've never sat on a board on which the CEO was coddled by the investors or directors. When there was good news in our board meetings, I saw applause and gratitude. When there was bad news, I witnessed anger and shame. It's the CEO's job, along with his or her executive team, to buffer the rest of the company from these closed-door emotions while dealing proactively with the underlying issues.

As stated repeatedly in this book, transparency is important for a love-based culture, so I'm not suggesting that you shouldn't share the challenges facing your company with your management or with your employees. Rather, take care that the emotions that accompany bad news are used judiciously. Fear and an angry boss are temporary motivators at best.

Remember, the way that leaders respond to their employees impacts the way they act in turn. A company can't inhabit the seventh principle of winning overall if we talk the talk of love but then operate out of a place of anger and fear in the long term.

One of the most powerful words on the pyramid chart a few pages back is "forgiveness." When you forgive, you let go of the lower emotions of fear.

Forgiveness is rarely woven into a company's culture. Instead, a focus on forms and protocols that highlight an employee's shortcomings can create a discouraging atmosphere, one that is fearful of idleness and of legal liability. In the end, this punitive atmosphere creates discord and separation as employees distance themselves from their peers who have been in the wrong.

Fishbowl Inventory, a tax management software company, realized this and did away with punitive red tape in favor of a system of trust and forgiveness. As a result, says its president, Mary Michelle Scott, the company has "sales reps who have been here for a decade, support techs who have been here 8+ years, and 25-year-olds who state flat-out that they never intend to leave."[10]

> ## "The weak can never forgive. Forgiveness is the attribute of the strong."
> MAHATMA GANDHI

The benefits of forgiving an employee for a shortcoming, whether it's coming in late or not closing a big client deal, has a greater impact even than improving your company's culture. As an added bonus, according to the Mayo Clinic, letting go of grudges and bitterness can make way for improved health and peace of mind.

Forgiveness can lead to:

» Healthier interpersonal relationships

» Improved mental health

» Less anxiety, stress, and hostility

» Lower blood pressure

» Fewer symptoms of depression

» A stronger immune system

» Improved heart health

» Improved self-esteem

How's that for the benefits of a love-based culture?

Whether you are a manager or an employee, every day you have the choice to operate either in the lower-level emotions of anger or fear or the higher-level emotions of forgiveness and trust. Neither forgiveness nor trust mean that you agree with the mistakes others have made. They simply mean that you chose to take the high road and let go of the negative feelings that were bogging you down.

After all, your energy is better spent elsewhere.

PRINCIPLE #7

WINNING
Feel the Buzz of Success

The only alternative to winning is to lose, and when you consistently lose, you go out of business. There's a level of toughness in business that sometimes requires us to move faster than employees feel comfortable or to avert a crisis. All of us will feel this stress, but it's important that we return to love once the crisis is averted rather than live in chronic fear. Successfully navigating the maze between stress and love results in winning. When you win over and over and over, a contagious buzz grows. It makes every employee in the company feel like a winner.

Call to Action:

» Do you feel like a winner when you go to work everyday?

» Do you feel stress because you don't want to let your teammates down, or do you feel it because of the chronic fear being passed down the org chart?

» Do customers reach out to your company because they want to work with the best? Do you make them feel like they are a part of a special family?

» When have you experienced "acute" fear in the workplace? Was it helpful to you? If not, how could you have shifted your mindset to make it better?

» Do you have any employees that do not fit within the love-based culture you encourage in your place of work? If so, what is your tough-love strategy for approaching the situation?

My Lessons Learned:

» I frequently felt anger as a CEO. That anger was based on the passion I had for our company. My anger created fear for others, though. At times that was needed to move faster or to solve a crisis, but I had to be constantly mindful that, if not checked, my anger could create a fear-based company.

» Fear of failure is an internal driver for highly motivated people. That's very different from the chronic fear propagated by fear-based companies.

» Tough love is still love. Handling tough people problems while showing them the dignity they deserve will either result in an employee who turns around their performance or who is terminated from the company.

» Do your best to follow HR guidelines, but once your gut makes a decision, follow it.

ACTS OF LOVE

I had just given birth to my second son. It was a very traumatic delivery that had people worried for a while.

My boss was at a huge conference when I went into labor and was having some very important meetings, but that didn't stop her from checking in for updates very often. At one point I thought she might even fly home just to make sure I was okay.

Even though she had spent exhausting and long hours on her feet, away from her own family, as soon as she was back in town, she came to see me and my baby in the hospital. I'll never forget her holding my newborn! The fact that she had time to stop and get me the softest pajamas that I still wear to this day is just a bonus.

8

THE THREE Ps:
Hardwire Processes to Trust

If you want to move the needle of your company toward love, you may need to change more about your business than you realize. Many of the core processes, policies, and procedures within your organization will need to be evaluated.

HARDWIRE PROCESSES TO TRUST

The rubber meets the road with HR policies and procedures. Like fear-based companies, love-based companies design their policies and procedures to protect them from regulatory requirements, but they also create these procedures with an assumption that they can trust their employees to make responsible decisions, instead of enforcing strict rules with associated penalties to protect the company. Just as importantly, a love-based company's employees trust their managers to provide them with subjective, real-time feedback.

Trusting employees is a simple, fundamental difference between HR policies and procedures in a love-based company and HR policies and procedures in a fear-based company.

LOVE OR FEAR? CARROTS OR STICKS?

I worked with a company whose fear-based process for business travel worked like this:

- » You must stay in one of these hotels (i.e., generally Marriott, Hilton, or Hyatt).

- » If you don't, regardless of the price of your stay, you will be given a "violation."

- » If you accumulate X number of violations, you will not get a bonus.

Our team hated this policy because they could almost always find hotels that were not only cheaper, but also more convenient to the project site to which they were assigned. Undoubtedly, this policy was in place because of a corporate rate some HR manager was very proud to have negotiated. It also had likely been put in place because a few employees had abused the company's money.

Alternatively, in Healthlink's love-based culture, our people not only saved us money because of their extreme desire to be frugal, but also called out their peers when they saw inappropriate spending behavior. We even extended this philosophy to how we negotiated reimbursed travel expenses by moving to a fixed per diem that ultimately cost our customers less money. When we trusted our employees to do the right thing, they did.

In short, love-based companies trust their team members to spend money like it is their own. Fear-based companies assume employees can't be trusted and that money is their primary motivator. While money may well be the primary motivator in some jobs, people who work in environments in which they must depend on others to succeed place a high value on relationships. Love-based cultures not only recognize this fact but also design their processes, policies, and procedures to encourage trust and teamwork. This fundamental difference has as much to do with driving the culture of the company as Acts of Love, compassionate leadership, core values, or a higher calling.

ENCOURAGING LOVE-BASED POLICIES AND PROCEDURES

The world of HR policies, compensation programs, and other management processes is ever-changing as innovative new ideas become fashionable. As such, I don't have canned processes or policies that will find the love-based holy grail for you. What's important is that no policy puts individual accomplishments above the team's or the company's success and that every policy defaults to trusting the employee within boundaries as long as they comply with regulatory requirements.

If you have control over your company's processes, try reviewing them through the following filters:

» Does this process promote teamwork?

» Does it encourage people to work together rather than independently?

» Do your leadership training programs actively support a love-based culture?

» Do you allow critical decisions to be made in the field by employees who work closely with clients?

» Do performance appraisals enable managers to improve their employees' self-awareness?

» Are incentives designed to help the employee focus on adding value to the overall company first and their personal goals second?

» Do employees feel comfortable raising their hands to identify problems early in the process without fear of retribution?

Be aware that some policies are the direct result of governmental regulatory requirements, in which case your company has no choice but to follow the law of the land. In most other cases, though, the leadership of the company can make these decisions, which have a significant influence on all aspects of the business, from training to performance appraisals.

The following are policies and procedures that we at Healthlink consciously formed to embody our love-based culture. If you're in a position to influence the policies, processes, and procedures at your company, whether directly or indirectly as a suggestion to the HR department, I hope you'll start with these.

Respect Employee Surveys

The devil is in the details, so doing a deep dive into every corner of how a management system supports and even creates culture is very important. The only way to know if you're moving in the right direction is by asking.

Start with your employees. Conduct annual employee surveys with a focus on culture. It's important to know if you are living your corporate values authentically. It's also important to know what policies and procedures or internal processes are causing more harm than good.

Healthlink took these surveys seriously and had them professionally administered by a third party to make sure they were free of bias. The results gave us insight into critical areas, both within the organizational chart and throughout the company. It told us where we needed to focus. After conducting a critical analysis of the problems that the survey identified, we formed teams of employees to better understand the issues and to develop solutions. Both the survey results and ensuing solutions were transparent to our employees. Each year we would resurvey the problems identified the year before to make sure we were improving and not accepting anything less than forward motion on any issue.

Any leader that doesn't do this every year, if not more often, is flying their business blindly. They're like the emperor with no clothes, not wanting to disrupt the comfort of their corner office with inconvenient truths that are right under their nose. Being self-aware as a leader and as an entire company is critical in the move to a love-based culture. Employees need to see tough problems being solved by caring leaders whom they know are looking out for their best interests. A survey is a strong way to put this in place.

Promote Team Hiring

One process that supported a strong, love-based culture at Healthlink was team hiring. In team hiring, several people on the team that has the vacancy are involved in the hiring process, not just the hiring manager. One employee involved in the process may not know anything about the skills the candidate needs for the job but will still be able to evaluate the potential hire for their fit within the company culture. This person protects the culture and is adamant about not allowing even one bad apple into the company. This type of team player is priceless. They may not be the highest-ranked sales producer, but they are the bond that holds the company culture together.

I called these protectors of our culture angels, and I can still identify them today. There were numerous occasions when the angels would not hire someone that I had referred to the company. They didn't care if the person was referred by the CEO or by anyone else. Their job was to protect our way of doing business, even if it meant saying no to me.

On a couple of occasions, I overruled the team and hired the candidate anyway. One of those hires turned into a superstar; the other was a bomb, and I paid dearly for overruling the team. While the bomb was highly competent, he wasn't a cultural fit for the company and should not have been hired. Since I had overruled a team of people, some of whom had to work for him, he had no buy-in from the start. The very culture I had implemented defeated me.

We also gave our internal team of recruiters veto power over any candidate, even if that candidate had passed a team interview. Our recruiters saw behavior that sometimes wasn't identified during the interview process. I remember one promising candidate who had breezed through the process until one of the recruiters called to plan her final interview. During the conversation, the candidate became rude and demanded a first-class aisle seat on her flight to the final interview as well as someone to pick her up at the airport.

Once that story was shared, we all knew the recruit was dead in the water. Those entitled behaviors hadn't shown up in the initial interview process, including the one with the team, but once exposed? Bye-bye, candidate.

Unlock Open-Door Policies

One of the most important policies to establish in a love-based company is a true open-door policy.

Back when I was a low-level manager at EDS, I received an email addressed to all managers from the CEO, Mort Meyerson. It defined the open-door policy for EDS: "Any employee of EDS can talk to any manager with no concerns of retribution." Under this quote was the simple statement: "Any manager who chooses to not comply with this policy will be terminated from the company." Two sentences. That was it.

> I called these protectors of our culture angels, and I can still identify them today. There were numerous occasions when the angels would not hire someone that I had referred to the company. They didn't care if the person was referred by the CEO or by anyone else. Their job was to protect our way of doing business, even if it meant saying no to me.

Mort's email was cut and dry because that was all it needed to be. Either your door is open under all conditions, or it's not. There is no in between. What if you knew, as an employee at any level, that you could walk into the office of the president of your company without fear of reprisal? That employee might feel that it was worth letting the president know about an idea he's had to provide better, more cost-effective service to a client or that it was worth sharing any potential problems within the organization. Having the freedom to talk to the CEO might mean that someone with an idea for a new product or service could pitch it without going through the formal process of making an appointment, creating a presentation, and then deciding not to go through with it after all because the stakes had become too high. Sometimes an informal conversation is much more valuable than an "official" one.

Lots of companies talk about being transparent and accessible but don't walk the talk. Few have an open-door policy that focuses on caring, respect, and open and honest feedback that's supported by accessibility and rooted in love. At EDS, I also knew that I needed to be ready for a potentially painful conversation. If I used the open-door policy to communicate to any manager in the company, I needed to be ready for a response that might not be what I expected or wanted to hear.

In many company cultures, employees know that if they speak up, their ideas will get shot down, criticized, or ignored. In some companies, speaking up means risking getting fired, especially if the employee is outspoken or if it's perceived that the employee is revealing bad practices, processes, systems, or any view that goes against the grain of existing management. Why would anyone in a fear-based culture take that risk? When employees at any level are afraid to speak up to present new ideas or reveal dents in the system, problems continue to grow.

Why are employees afraid? "In a phrase, self-preservation," wrote two professors in an article for the *Harvard Business Review*. "While it's obvious why employees fear bringing up certain issues, such as whistle-blowing, we found the innate protective instinct so powerful that it also inhibited speech that clearly would have been intended to help the organization."[1]

Open and honest communication is the key to a love-based culture. So, how do you ensure that your employees can act in love instead of responding in fear, remaining quiet about dirty secrets and bad managers? How can any businesses improve if they never learn about their problems?

VOICE OF DANA

Ivo and I weren't the only people who defended our culture. Healthlink's open-door policy was an important element that allowed employees to raise concerns about things that violated our core values. Healthlink was a virtual company; employees lived and worked all over the country. How do you have a meaningful open-door policy in that environment?

The way we did it was simple: if an employee wanted to talk to any manager, our commitment was that we'd find a way to meet face to face within two business days. I had people come to me with concerns, ideas, and frequently an offer to help solve an issue. Whether it was a proposal writer who felt that a sales team was overcommitting, or an employee who felt mistreated by a manager, our virtual doors were always open, and there was never any recrimination for the thoughts or feelings expressed there.

Remember That Love Has No Bias

At Healthlink, we reviewed our benefits program every year. In the late 1990s, we were going through our annual review and, for the third year in a row, considered whether to award benefits to same-sex couples. Our criterion was whether it made business sense to offer benefits to gay couples who were not legally married. In the preceding two years, the benefits review committee had declined to support same-sex benefits.

In the third year, though, the committee recommended that we offer same-sex benefits. They had concluded that if we could figure out how to handle the legal issues surrounding the "not-married" part of the matter, the advantages to the company would be greater than the disadvantages. This was not a social issue but a business issue that required careful analysis. I read the committee's thoughtful presentation and agreed. In the 1990s, very few companies offered same-sex benefits, and as much as I'd like to say that I was being a progressive, forward-thinking leader, the fact is that I was only thinking about what was best overall for the company.

During those early years, our company's name was IMG. After IMG acquired another company called Healthlink, we changed our name to Healthlink (much better name). Years later, one of our employees told me that within our gay-employee community, IMG had stood for "I Am Gay." I asked why and learned that we were known for being gay-friendly. I had no idea. I had just been doing what was of value to my company but was pleased that those decisions had led to this reputation.

Although the conclusion to offer same-sex benefits pertained only to LGBTQ+ couples, the baseline concept extends beyond that. The workplace needs to be a safe haven for everyone. Religion, race, sex, other individual characteristics, none of those matter. What matters is that our policies toward all groups make us feel like a love-based company.

I remember once interviewing a woman for a manager position. I asked her why she wanted to work for Healthlink. She said that we had a good distribution of female leaders, and she didn't want to work for a company that had a glass ceiling. Her comment caused me to pause. I pulled an organizational chart out of my desk and started counting the male and female boxes. She was right; there were more women in leadership positions than there were men, including among my direct reports.

> In the 1990s, very few companies offered same-sex benefits, and as much as I'd like to say that I was being a progressive, forward-thinking leader, the fact is that I was only thinking about what was best overall for the company.

While I'm not opposed to some of the regulatory requirements or guidelines prescribing ratios for gender parity in the workplace, I question whether they are really needed in a love-based culture. I may be naïve in thinking that hiring, promoting, and compensating employees can be fair to all; I'm sure that good ol' boy networks thrive in many companies. But in a love-based company, what matters when you hire someone is the expectation that they will do the job well and fit within your company culture. Gender shouldn't have any impact on those determinations.

Though Healthlink had a good distribution of male and female employees, we did not have a good mix of races. We could have done better on that score. Of the over 20 business and nonprofit boards I've been on over the years, most were dominated by white men. That's not to say that the companies they represented weren't gender-balanced, but at the governance level, they were not. It was certainly not because white men are better at business, so we obviously still have a long way to go.

Implement Love-Based Processes In New-Employee Orientation

I remember reading a definition that has stuck with me. "Orientation" was originally defined as "facing east," as in the direction from which the sun rises. (It also has religious implications, but that's not what I'm talking about here.) In the practice of yoga, the sun provides light as well as the start of a new day. It is worth remembering that we start every day with the opportunity to do good and do well. Every day, we can renew our intentions to provide the best service to our customers and to value our colleagues. That's quite relevant when introducing new employees to the unique attributes of a love-based culture.

VOICE OF DANA

Ivo has said that you must rethink everything you do if you want to create a love-based culture. One area to look at is how you bring new employees on board. A lot of companies view orientation as a time to train employees on how to report their time and expenses, introduce HR policies and business rules, and even provide product and services training. Healthlink had a different idea.

Our orientation lasted a full week. Sure, we covered a few things about expense reporting and how to use our internal systems, but by far, the majority of the time was spent on understanding our "culture." We explained the technique we used to start meetings with a core-value discussion. We taught new employees that anyone could raise their hand if they had a concern about a project, and we explained our open-door policy. Because teamwork was such an integral part of our culture, we spent a lot of time discussing how highly effective teams function, and we practiced team tools such as meeting facilitation and brainstorming. We had other classes that taught specialized subjects, but every employee, no matter their job, had to attend this orientation.

Here's what's really interesting: occasionally we'd have an urgent client need and would allow a new employee to skip orientation to go straight to a project. After reviewing hundreds of new hires, we found that most of the employees who left the company within their first year were employees who had been allowed to skip orientation.

When people understand right off the bat that the company has a higher calling, a commitment to quality, and that they are part of a team that cares about and values them, they feel loyalty and a sense of belonging from the very start. An employee orientation that focuses on values and culture is good for business and is a critical element for success in a love-based culture.

Dana's observations about those who skipped orientation versus those who completed it are spot-on.

I once had a manager working for me who was revered as a thought leader and an icon in our industry. Dignitaries from foreign countries sought her out for advice. She was a frequent speaker at conferences and commanded a large sum of money for corporate appearances. I was responsible for giving her an appraisal.

In preparation, I solicited feedback from both her customers and her employees. Customers raved about her and appreciated the wisdom she contributed. The sales team loved her because she was impressive on sales calls and would help them close deals. The small group of people who worked directly for her, however, were not so complimentary. They felt she was arrogant, didn't listen, and, even worse, didn't care. They were offended that she didn't lead with love in the spirit of the company.

Her opinion of herself was high. She assumed that her team would bow down to her the same way that her customers did. She felt like they were lucky to have someone as great as she was rather than a nobody in the industry as their manager.

When I gave her her appraisal, I complimented her work in the field and let her know that her contribution to sales was valuable to the company. I then told her that her reputation as a thought leader did not extend to her ability to lead her team. They needed her to be a real person who cared about them rather than rest on her laurels as an industry icon. She was a little put off by the conversation, but it was one that needed to take place.

I watched her over the next few months and didn't see any change in her behavior. Through walking around making idle chatter, I took the temperature of her team. I got the impression that they felt she was not changing either.

After a few more conversations, I told her that despite the value she brought to our company, how much she brought in in revenue, and how she enhanced our reputation in the industry by association, she could not stay with the company. As I discussed in chapter 7, maintaining the culture was far more critical and had far greater benefits than her individual contribution, as good as it was. I prided myself on being direct yet tactful when conducting these conversations. She clearly got the point, and while it hurt her ego, she accepted the feedback. Deep down in her heart, she knew that she didn't fit. We ended our conversation in a spirit of mutual respect. She respected my honest and candid feedback, and I appreciated her willingness to be open and listen.

I helped her get another job that was better suited to her ego, so she landed on her feet. The company, however, was blown away that we would release someone who had had so much external value for being a disaster internally. Of course, as leaders, we couldn't discuss any of the details of the separation, but her team knew. Word spread. We had chosen to value her team members and our culture over the superstar's metrics. Her separation reinforced that no single person was bigger than our company culture. Once again, love prevailed.

BRINGING IT ALL TOGETHER WITH THE THREE Ps

It may be growing clear now that the 10 principles of a love-based culture function at their most efficient when they work in tandem with one another. Nowhere is this clearer than in the implementation of policies, processes, and procedures that prop up love-based compensation, permit authentic leadership, and, as we'll see in the following chapter, allow enough trust for employees to make command decisions in the field.

As you move forward in your love-based journey, I hope that you'll block out some time to speak with those in charge of the three Ps in your company. My personal experience, and that of so many others, tells me you won't regret it.

PRINCIPLE #8

The Three Ps:
Policies, Processes, Performance
Hardwire Processes to Trust

Love-based companies design their operating policies and procedures with an assumption that they can trust their employees to "do what's right" within predetermined boundaries. These boundaries will vary based on the size of the company, whether it's public or private, if it's under government contracts or regulations, and so on. Regardless of size, love-based companies believe that employees will spend the company's money responsibly, like it is their own. They believe that their orientation and training programs are as much about culture as they are about the employee handbook.

Call to Action:

» Do the policies in your company trust you to do what's right, or penalize you for doing what's wrong?

» Do you trust your manager to have an honest conversation with you during your performance appraisal, even if they show some tough love?

» Are you appraised based on your overall contribution to the company, much of which cannot be measured?

» Does your company have an open-door policy? If not, is there some way you can suggest it to your direct manager or to HR?

» Do more people than the hiring manager have a say in recruiting new employees?

» Do new hires in your company learn your mission statement and core values, or just day-to-day logistics?

162

My Lessons Learned:

» Employee surveys will give you the (sometimes-painful) information you need to move your company toward love.

» Teams of peers should make hiring decisions, not individual managers. I did at times overrule team decisions, despite knowing the possible repercussions.

» Open-door policies need to be clearly stated and repeated over time. Managers who don't respect this policy or show retribution to employees who use it should be terminated.

» Onboarding for new hires should be equally focused on culture and skills.

ACTS OF LOVE

At a previous employer, my coworker's wife has been diagnosed with a very serious form of cancer. They had 3 kids, who were then 18 months, 3 years, and 4 years old.

After using all of his holidays and legal time to take care of his wife, my coworker was facing the dilemma of either quitting the job to take care of her—therefore losing the only income in the household—or to keep working and therefore not be around his wife and kids very much.

All of the company's employees (including executives) agreed to give him one of our own vacation days to help. The CEO then decided that every day given would count for the giver as only half a day, while for our coworker it would count as two days. Thanks to that Act of Love, my coworker was able to take nine months of paid time off to take care of his wife.

To this day, I wish I could find another workplace where humanity is the primary focus, where we are all there to help each other, and where we feel like a true family.

9

DECISION-MAKING:
Empower Those Closest to the Customer to Do What's Right

I had a friend who took on a CEO role for a large insurance company. Only six months later, he resigned. I was shocked and asked him what had happened. He said that he was a "growth" CEO. Once he dug under the covers of his new employer, he concluded that what they needed was a "turnaround" CEO. Different flavor, different skills. He told the board they had made a mistake in hiring him, and he would help them find the right replacement.

It's rare to see founder-CEOs grow their companies from zero revenue to billions. In fact, according to David Friedberg, founder of WeatherBill (now known as the Climate Corporation), a weather insurance website, "There's a 0.00006% chance of building a company that will grow to be worth more than a billion dollars."[1] The implication is that the complementary side of that percentage represents companies that don't make it.

I'm in the club of CEOs who have built $100 million companies that got acquired. I've been the executive chairman and director of other companies that achieved the same goal. None made it all the way to $1 billion of revenue.

It was a real-time education to understand that the love-based leader I needed to be at $1 million in revenue was very different from the one I needed to be at $100 million. If the company had not been acquired and I had continued to build it to $1 billion in revenue, I would have had to change even more, or likely would have been fired along the way for not being a good fit to run that large of a company.

> "The only reason you don't come to a consensus on solving a problem is that you either haven't worked an issue hard or long enough, or you don't have the right people in the room to engage in the conversation."
>
> ROD CANION

I've worked with numerous start-ups that hired experienced executives from big companies, from divisions that pulled in over $500 million in revenue. I can't think of a single executive of this description who succeeded in their new role. The skills required to run a half-billion-dollar division of a large corporation are different than the ones required to start a new company or even help an early-stage company grow. Many executives assume that because they have made money at one level, they must be great business people who can succeed at all levels. I have sadly watched many experience their first defeat at the helm of tiny companies.

As companies move from one step to the next and executives move in and out of the corner office, it's inevitable that the personal touch of the original love-based culture will evolve and become dependent on new processes, methodologies, and organizational models to keep up with the company's growth.

It is during this growth transition that many companies lose their love-based roots and move the needle on the Love/Fear Continuum toward fear. Professional managers replace founders, and metrics replace leadership. Becoming efficient can become a higher priority than having the personal touch that characterized the smaller love-based culture. But fear doesn't develop overnight; it creeps in one change at a time.

PRINCIPLE #9

DECISION-MAKING
Empower Those Closest to the Customer to Do What's Right

In my first CEO position in the early 1990s, I had a board made up mostly of former Compaq executives. Many of the tenets of our love-based culture were formed by our board, who had all grown up in love-based cultures themselves. Under the leadership of Rod Canion, Compaq had become the fastest-growing company in the history of business for many years ($100 million in year one; $1 billion in year four). They invented portable computing in the 1980s by creating one of the first computers that could fit into the overhead bin on an airplane. It was a "luggable" computer, way bigger than today's laptops.

What few people outside of Texas know is that this company had a love-based culture that enabled them to experience hyper-growth while being considered the very best place to work in Houston. While Rod is known as an industry icon for his feats at Compaq, he is also a legend to many a Compaq employee.

Rod's personal philosophy was, "The only reason you don't come to a consensus on solving a problem is that you either haven't worked an issue hard or long enough, or you don't have the right people in the room to engage in the conversation." Time after time, Dana, the rest of the team, and I would come to these early Healthlink board meetings and watch the masters at work, solving problems to the benefit of the company. It was inspiring to see those dynamics operate at the board level.

However, for all that a board should do to govern from a place of love (see chapter 5 for more information), it is also crucial that love-based governance take place within lower-level teams.

TRUSTING EMPLOYEES TO MAKE COMMAND DECISIONS

When Healthlink began to grow larger, I believed that we could provide higher-quality service if we made decisions quickly and at the grassroots level, where employees were closer to the customers and better understood the problems that needed to be solved. The less bureaucracy there was, the faster decisions could be made.

As the CEO, I was always in push, push, push mode. I couldn't go fast enough and hated the "organization" getting in my way. I wanted to make decisions, put a plan together, and go, go, go. My problem was my COO, who kept reminding me that my great ideas needed to be implemented by real people. These real people not only needed to understand the problem we were solving but also wanted to be involved in developing the solution.

Time and time again, I'd make decisions and start to push only to hit what I lovingly referred to as the "Dana Wall." When I used my force of personality to push an initiative forward, I'd watch it fizzle to a slow death. Meanwhile, I'd see the decisions implemented under Dana's teamwork method slowly build steam, ending up with the entire company on board and owning the solution.

I learned from Dana that building a love-based culture was often about respecting the great people we hired and using them to make the company even better. Within a system of predetermined guidelines that protected the company as a whole, employees were permitted to make command decisions if it would be the right thing to do for the customer. In other situations, decisions that didn't have a looming deadline were discussed internally and often put to a vote. As much as my primal instincts wanted to go fast, "fast enough" was usually not only the better approach but also absolutely required. Once Dana had the entire company operating as a well-oiled machine, I had no choice but to do things her way. The lesson here is that, often, a CEO striving for efficiency can become the very bottleneck they're trying to avoid. The love-based culture of teamwork was stronger than me alone, and that was how it should be.

What resulted was less bureaucracy, which allowed for higher-quality decisions to be made, which I'd wanted in the first place. The collateral benefit of having employees in the field who were empowered to make decisions was that the customer developed confidence in the leaders that were their primary connection to the company. If there was a problem, they would tell the people they worked with every day, and the problem would be resolved without having a chance to fester.

Customers liked knowing that they were dealing with a decision-maker rather than some low-level minion who had to ask their boss for permission every time there was a problem.

VOICE OF DANA

Ivo always wanted to go fast, fast, fast, but I had to make sure we had solid processes and good discipline in place. A great example of how these two forces came together was around decision-making. At one point, Healthlink had become big and bureaucratic. We'd encountered a period of the blahs. Sales were slow, energy was down, and the outlook was pessimistic. It took forever to make a decision, and our customers could tell we weren't as nimble as we once had been. We needed to get our swagger back. We needed to get into action mode!

We agreed to move decision-making closer to the client so that we could eliminate time-consuming delays waiting for a decision from "corporate." But that idea was scary. When the company was small, Ivo and I had been involved in almost every decision that took place. Could we trust our people in the field to make good decisions?

The solution was simple. We created a framework called "The Rules of the Road" to guide decision-making. These rules gave our people in the field guidance on a wide range of decisions, from pricing and staffing to capital purchases and contract negotiations. We based this framework on our understanding of risk; where there was little risk, our client-facing team could make decisions on the spot.

Trust-Based Decision-Making

Top-Level Decision-Making

The change to our business was startling. People in the field felt empowered and emboldened. Customers liked the new, responsive, nimble Healthlink. The excitement felt throughout the company was contagious.

Ivo got what he wanted: we moved a lot faster. And I got what I wanted: we were still operating in a disciplined, structured way that limited risk and ensured good outcomes. We were able to do this because we had an environment of trust. We trusted people in the field to do what was right and to make good decisions, and they trusted us to support the decisions they had made. All it took to get us out of the doldrums was a good dose of trust, a little love, and some solid rules of the road.

★ ★ ★

EFFICIENT DECISION-MAKING IN MEDIUM- AND LARGE-SIZED BUSINESSES

What can you do to encourage your team to speak up and present their ideas? There are a million books out there on how to capture those great ideas that fuel innovation in the workplace, but when fear is in the air, those ideas never get captured. Once again, trust becomes an asset to the company. In a love-based culture in which employees have no fear of retribution or worry of offending their boss, great ideas can emerge.

You may recall the *Harvard Business Review* survey of corporate culture from chapter 8. In it, half the respondents revealed that they felt it was not "safe to speak up" or challenge tradition. What they were most reticent to talk about were not problems but creative ideas for improving products, process-es, or performance. Why? "[T]he perceived risks of speaking up felt very personal and immediate to employees, whereas the possible future benefit to the organization from sharing their ideas was uncertain. So, people often instinctively played it safe by keeping quiet. Their frequent conclusion seemed to be, 'When in doubt, keep your mouth shut.'"[2]

I was once in a meeting at Healthlink in which we discussed why it took so long for projects to be completed. One of the par-ticipants said, "Our biggest problem is getting decisions from all of the executives. They're busy."

> We've all heard the term "too big to fail," but can companies grow too big to love?

Another person immediately suggested, "Why don't we get them all in the same room at the same time and present the decisions, discuss issues, and get commitments before they leave the room?"

Thus, Decision Day was born. It became a core part of how we completed every project. It cut project times in half and resulted in much better decisions since all of our executives could hear the pros and cons at the same time. Something as simple as setting up a meeting to solicit decisions dramatically improved the process, but it wouldn't have emerged had we not had a culture in which everyone felt comfortable to raise their hand and throw out a solution.

SCALING UP: HOW BIG IS TOO BIG TO LOVE?

We've all heard the term "too big to fail," but can companies grow too big to love? A frequent comment I receive when I talk to my peers about a love-based culture is that it can't work in major corporations. I would argue that it most certainly can and does.

I have provided supporting information from and about the executives of major international corporations to assert that none of my 10 Principles of a Love-Based Culture need necessarily fail in a multibillion-dollar company.

10 PRINCIPLES OF A LARGE ENTERPRISE'S LOVE-BASED CULTURE

100% Referenceability - You may remember Volvo Vision 2020 from chapter 1. In it, Håkan Samuelsson, president and CEO of Volvo Cars, stated: "Our vision is that by 2020 no one should be killed or seriously injured in a new Volvo car." Volvo Cars brings in $50B+ in annual revenue. It is a division of Volvo, itself a $300B+ company, and still sets aggressive quality goals.

Leadership - Louis V. Gerstner, Jr., the former CEO of IBM, once said: "Until I came to IBM, I probably would have told you that culture was just one among several important elements in any organization's makeup and success—along with vision, strategy, marketing, financials, and the like. I came to see, in my time at IBM, that culture isn't just one aspect of the game. It is the game. In the end, an organization is nothing more than the collective capacity of its people to create value."[3]

Core Values - According to Ward Nye, CEO of Martin Marietta, a building materials company and part of the S&P 500: "You make sure people are hearing [about your core values] from every level of the organization and you live it every day. Living it, not talking about it, is what really makes the big difference."[4]

A Higher Calling - It is part of Salesforce's mission to improve not just their company, but the community around them as well. At an employee's first day of work, they perform community service in the afternoon by going to a homeless shelter, hospital, or public school.[5]

Governance - The board of directors at Compaq Computers used its meetings as working sessions to solve problems. Unfortunately, most big-company board meetings are dominated by impressive status reports. Is it impossible to incorporate problem-solving at the top of an international corporation? Of course not. Many great companies are governed by board members who represent divergent views and work together to solve problems that impact everyone.

Compensation - Love-based compensation can be much more difficult for big companies to implement due to regulatory compliance and threats of discrimination. Even if that is the case, many big companies have moved away from individual incentive-based compensation programs to rewarding people based on their contribution to their team's success.

Winning - Can you walk into a big company and feel the buzz? The buzz is the result of happy employees working for a company that is winning in the market. The stock of Glassdoor's Best Places to Work award winners, which are recognized for their high employee satisfaction, regularly outperforms the market by 2.8 times.[6] Most of these were large, publicly traded companies.

The 3 Ps: Policies, Processes, Performance - Believe it or not, 360-degree reviews are common in big companies. Many firms, like PwC, are moving away from a number scale rating to setting discussions around individual and team performance goals.[7]

Decision-Making - It takes a special CFO to create processes that allow decisions to be made by the employees who are closest to the client. Big companies have greater risks. Releasing control requires boundaries, but also fuels faster growth.

Acts of Love - Acts of Love are common in big companies. Many of those documented in this book come from larger businesses.

As you can see, no fewer than 7 of the 10 principles are no-brainers, even at the multibillion-dollar level. What's more, with open communication and effort among HR, finance, and operational compliance departments, governance, compensation, and decision-making can move from fear to love on a grand corporate scale, too.

EMBRACING RISKY DECISIONS

At 3M, it was hard to get promoted without having made a highly visible mistake that was widely discussed. This was not because 3M loved mistakes but because the company valued risk-taking, which they knew was the spark for innovation.[8]

For instance, 3M engineer Richard Drew inadvertently invented Scotch tape while trying to solve a tape problem for painters of the then-fashionable two-tone look on automobiles.

What's more, a mistake coupled with the frustration of a choir singer led to the invention of one of the most basic modern-day office supplies: Post-It notes. Spencer Silver, a 3M chemist, accidentally invented the insufficiently sticky stuff while trying to create a strong adhesive for the aerospace industry. Years later, the resulting weak—and at that point, use-less—adhesive was used by Art Fry, another 3M chemist, who was frustrated at having his paper bookmarks fall out of his choir hymnal. He affixed Silver's adhesive to the back of his bookmarks and Post-It notes were born.[9] Without 3M's culture of innovation and its acceptance of mistakes, some of the most famous products of the last 100 years might never have been invented.

Making decisions involves risk. In most businesses, risk is terrible. Risk gets people fired. Manage to the downside of risk 100% of the time, and you have no risk, right?

Wrong. Risk drives growth. If you're not pushing the envelope and taking chances on growing sales, adding new products, or entering new markets, then you have no chance to grow revenue. In a fear-based company, risk creates fear, which is then managed by an inordinate amount of bureaucracy.

All the additional processes that are put in place to make decisions risk-free actually increase risk. The time and angst that accompany this excessive bureaucracy create inefficiencies that increase the probability of failure. A love-based company will make decisions fully understanding the risk, and trust those responsible to execute and communicate so that risk is minimized.

A more ideal way to reduce excessive risk is to have an early warning system in place. Our employees in the field knew that their goal was to have all our customers be 100% referenceable. For them to succeed, they needed to have control over the quality of the services they provided and the decisions that went along with that responsibility. In a love-based culture, employees feel comfortable alerting management to problems early, frequently even before the customer discovers the problem. They don't fear speaking up and do so with customer satisfaction in mind.

This way, whatever risk has been assumed can be swiftly extinguished. What does this mean to investors? Faster growth with less risk. When advantage slides over to those who take calculated risks, you'll have a company that enjoys the benefits of faster decisions, greater innovation, and far more satisfied customers.

THE DARK SIDE OF SOLO DECISIONS

Decision-making and mistakes are not always good things, though. One of the ways decision-making can lead to negative outcomes is if it is performed in a vacuum, without guidance from others, or, as I did in the following example, while ignoring the greater framework of a company's decision-making guidelines.

Healthlink once lost an IT-strategy deal to a much bigger competitor, which the prospective client had hired previously to do their strategic-market planning. Once the competitor completed the strategic plan, they used the executive relationships they had built to sell the information technology strategy project to the health system, too.

I was upset that a competitor who was far less qualified to handle IT strategy than Healthlink had swooped in and stolen a project that we believed was rightfully ours, even though we had not been selected nor did we have a contract. We did have a relationship with the client, just not the right one. After pondering the situation, I decided that we needed to expand to the strategic-market-planning business to make sure we didn't lose out on future opportunities.

I surveyed the industry and eventually acquired three boutique strategic planning companies. I architected and executed the acquisitions with Healthlink's CFO, and then made the biggest mistake of my career: I did not include my executive team in the decision-making process. Instead, I made a command decision.

Once the acquisition had been completed, some of the CEOs of the acquired companies joined Healthlink's executive management team. What ensued became the biggest lesson in my career.

It was a disaster.

The acquired executives didn't share the same set of values as Healthlink's original executive team. I gave these new executives a lot of leeway, and with it, they made some really bad decisions. Management meetings became contentious, and I found that I had to make command decisions, whereas previously the team would have reached a consensus. The business models of the strategic planning companies were different than ours, and Healthlink wasn't built to execute on multiple business models.

In one meeting, one of the acquired executives, Sally, had developed a list of strategic planning services Healthlink could take to market. All the managers were in the room, including her former boss Bill, who, it turned out, was her nemesis. Sally filled four whiteboards with list after list after list of services. When she was done, I counted the number of services Healthlink had to develop plans for; there were more services than we had employees. On top of that, as she went through her presentation, her nemesis sabotaged it line item by line item.

We were an hour into the meeting when I finally said, "Stop!" I looked around the room and told everyone to leave except Bill, to whom I said, "You, stay." Everyone sheepishly left. I looked at Bill and said, "This isn't working. You're going to have to go." Bill acted surprised and started rationalizing his behavior. I cut him off and said, "This isn't up for discussion. I've had enough. Please collect your things and leave now." Soon thereafter I also asked Sally to leave the company.

I then called a management meeting with only my top executives and apologized for the disrespect I had shown them in executing the acquisitions independently. I apologized for not seeking their advice, for not listening, and for not forming teams to help make these very important decisions. Over the next few months, I unwound all the acquisitions I had made and allowed the acquired employees and executives to return to the marketplace as independent companies.

While that mistake cost Healthlink a year of growth, I earned my Ph.D. in business in the process. The lessons learned from these failed acquisitions resulted in a list of services that could fit onto a Post-It note rather than the four full whiteboards Sally had proposed. The company had a strategic-planning focus. Finally.

The result was a very difficult and painful lesson about what happens when you forget your values, when you believe you are above everyone else, and when you personally experience culture slapping you so hard that it knocks you down.

During that period, which Dana and I considered the "dark days" of Healthlink, there was a chink in our armor. The Healthlink magic had faded, and we were, for a period of time, just another company with a CEO who spent his days soothing egos, fighting fires, and desperately trying to mentor people who had no desire to change. Every company has a defining moment in its life, and this was it both for Healthlink and for me as CEO. I was not being a love-based leader, not so much because of the way I treated people but because I had abandoned all the love-based principles I had helped create.

We all know that our greatest lessons come from our mistakes. In this case I made two mistakes: losing our focus on being the best at a few things rather than trying to master four whiteboards' worth of product solutions, and failing to respect a culture that I had helped to build—a culture that was inclusive, not exclusive; a culture in which trust was based on transparency, respect, and teamwork. The beauty of this lesson was that Healthlink's culture once again defeated me, the CEO. I was humbled but wiser. Much, much wiser.

This life lesson, along with a renewed focus on Healthlink's differentiating set of services thrust us into growth mode. There would be no more down years, no more dark days. No more questioning the values of the company. No more arrogance. Transparency, authenticity, open communication, and respect became renewed tenets of our love-based culture.

VOICE OF DANA

Ivo had a big "aha" moment when he dismantled the acquisitions he had made, and by acknowledging that he had learned from his mistake and apologizing to the company, he showed us a side of his character that I didn't usually see: someone who was humbled and vulnerable. Many members of the leadership team had felt betrayed when they were excluded from the decision-making process. I personally felt betrayed and wondered what I had done wrong to deserve to be locked out of such an important decision. I felt like I had been kicked off the island.

Ivo called us all into a room and told us he had made a mistake and apologized for not respecting the team. He admitted that in his desire to move fast he had violated a key tenet of our core values: teamwork. His apology and subsequent review of the lessons he had learned as a leader were heartfelt. My disappointment turned into a renewed passion for rebuilding our business. I had never doubted that Ivo's intention was to help the company, but his behavior was contrary to the culture we had all been involved in creating.

This may have been one of the single most important events in the company's history. We needed to go through this not only to test our culture but also to better focus the company, a much-needed adjustment to get us to the next level. We all learned from this experience, and the reunited team had an energy that enabled us to move rapidly to make the changes we needed to get the company back on target.

GREETING TRIUMPH AND FAILURE WITH TRUST, TRANSPARENCY, AND TRUTH

From top to bottom, love-based companies have authentic leaders who are real, make mistakes, and own up to them while encouraging their teams to do the same. Mistakes are a part of growth, and how you respond to them becomes a part of your love-based culture. Dana and I both knew we had to own up to our mistakes and be honest and transparent, whether it was with our employees or our customers.

Love-based companies have an open-door philosophy when it comes to sharing information with employees. At Health-link, we chose to be an open book for our workers. During our monthly employee teleconference calls, we disclosed the state of the business regardless of the impact it might have had on the people on the call. Our CFO always presented the financial statements on these calls without fear of judgment. If we had challenging projects, we discussed them openly. If the numbers were terrible, our people knew that we needed to tighten our belts.

We were equally transparent with our customers. Once we exceeded $50M in revenue, we started producing our version of an annual report. This document had the look and feel of a full-color, multi-page brochure with graphs and analysis. The content showed our revenue performance with some insights into our service lines. We also highlighted key employees and customers. Our goal was to keep our employees and customers up to date on who and what we were.

We purposely mailed this brochure to our employees' homes so that their family members could understand the company at which their spouse, child, or parent worked. It was my goal for this document to be displayed on their living room coffee tables. We also took the report to conferences and shared it with current and potential customers. It was not a salesy piece of collateral but rather a transparent document that gave the reader a chance to get to know who we really were.

Trust was integral to forming teams of people who felt like they had each other's backs and an environment in which there was no fear of raising one's hand to call out a troubled project. This allowed us to pull the right people together, at the right time, regardless of their position on the organizational chart, to provide what the customer needed.

This openness would not have worked outside of a love-based culture in which teamwork was paramount, and all employees, from the receptionist to the salespeople in the field, totally owned our commitment to customer satisfaction. It's remarkable how love-based decision-making, both for internal and customer-facing problems, can make even the largest steamer ship of a $500M company cruise along at a fair clip like it did in its speedboat start-up days.

Decision-making comes from a place of trust and love. If you trust that your employees will handle good or bad information responsibly, it's remarkable what solutions they'll come up with.

PRINCIPLE #9

DECISION-MAKING
Empower Those Closest to the Customer to Do What's Right

Trust employees who work closely with customers to make decisions, even if it costs the company money. Set and communicate boundaries to make sure your team members know what decisions can be made and, most importantly, that they are trusted to make a good decision.

Call to Action:

» If you are dealing with a tough customer issue, do you feel empowered to make decisions that may cost your company money, fully understanding that you must operate within predetermined boundaries?

» If you make a decision that turns out to be suboptimal, do you fear retribution from your company? Will you be punished? Or will you debrief with your leaders to better understand the lessons that need to be learned?

» Do you feel comfortable asking for help, regardless of the circumstances?

My Lessons Learned:

» For the person sitting on the other side of the desk from a client whose hair is on fire with anger, being empowered to make a decision that can defuse the situation is key. Waiting weeks for permission is the kiss of death for quality customer service. Trust those in the field to do what's right.

» When I empowered people in the field to make decisions, I also had to deal with some bad decisions being made. Mistakes are inevitable when risk is accepted as a necessary evil to grow one's business. I had to learn not to punish mistakes, but rather to use them to learn.

» The only reason a consensus can't be reached is either that you haven't worked on it long or hard enough, or that you don't have the right team working on the problem.

» Making solo decisions without the input of smart teammates is just flat-out stupid. Don't do it.

ACTS OF LOVE

My father passed away earlier this year after an extended illness. He was a small business owner for many years, and one of the stories shared at his funeral was how he would, without forethought and out of his generous and caring nature, pull cash out of his wallet and give it to an employee for doing a good job.

I later shared this with my leadership team as part of a reflection prior to the start of one of our team meetings. A few weeks later, the team surprised me with a box full of various gift cards. They had taken up a collection among themselves in honor of my dad, the thought being that I could hand them out to our associates on occasion just for doing a good job.

What a moving tribute to my dad's memory! I've truly enjoyed handing out these cards from time to time, and my associates really appreciate the personal recognition. It's a tradition that I plan to continue through my career in memory of my dad.

10

ACTS OF LOVE:
Show That You Care

By far, the 10th principle is the simplest thing anyone can do to move the needle on the Love/Fear Continuum closer to love: they can show kindness at work. This helps to say, "I care about you." More important than money, more important than performance metrics, showing that you care enough to do something special for an employee is what they will remember and treasure.

In the process of writing this book, I collected hundreds of Acts of Love in the workplace. Many made me smile; some brought a tear to my eye. There were common themes. The way that a company, and an employee's boss in particular, responded to a death in the family was a common one. Many of the letters dealt with the support people received when either they or a loved one had a health issue. Others reflected simple acts of recognition for a job well done. How easy is it to show this simple, human act of kindness? Many companies don't promote or support it, but individuals have the choice to do this themselves.

Developing a love-based culture isn't as easy as attending funerals or giving an employee extra time to be with sick parents or take care of children, but it's a start. It isn't necessary to completely dismantle a culture that has developed over decades. Instead, start by showing some compassion.

PRINCIPLE #10
ACTS OF LOVE
Show That You Care

I believe that most leaders have this compassion but have been brainwashed into believing that showing love in the workplace is a sign of weakness. The reality is that being open, transparent, and authentic requires a level of self-awareness that is uncompromising. Become that leader, and the strength of your leadership will be felt by all around you.

Within all the common themes of the letters, one of the most frequent phrases I read was "I will never forget." These words struck a chord with me. Some of these stories represented memories from more than 30 years ago, yet they are still as powerful today as when the Act of Love was performed. These lifelong memories were the result of someone in the company where the recipient of the kindness worked expressing love.

The major theme of all the letters was actually very simple: someone cared about me.

We all have patterns of behavior that become routine over time. Acts of Love get lost in the crisis of the day or in the many mundane tasks on our to-do lists. The stories that have been featured throughout this book are examples of how individual employers demonstrated love in a way that had an impact on an employee. Many of these Acts of Love are now memories that will never be forgotten.

VOICE OF DANA

While interviewing a nurse named Susan, I asked her why she wanted to work for Healthlink. Susan said that throughout her career she had wanted to make a difference by helping patients, but she found that as a nurse she could only help a handful of people at a time. So, she moved into her hospital's information systems department where she felt she could help all the nurses in her hospital take better care of patients by providing them with better information. By moving to Healthlink, Susan said, she could help hospitals across the country. She knew she couldn't help everyone personally, but through her actions she could touch people who could touch others, and eventually she believed she could make a huge difference. Her passion was contagious.

Susan's belief that her actions could impact many, many others has scientific support. In his book, The Tipping Point, Malcolm Gladwell gives examples of massive changes that started with the actions of a handful of people. He describes change as being like an epidemic: a few people's behavior can start to spread and grow exponentially. Once enough people adopt a new way of thinking or behaving (i.e., the tipping point), the change becomes common practice.

Gladwell gives the example of Hush Puppies shoes. Remember those? Hush Puppies were popular at one point, but by 1994 the brand was almost dead. Sales were down to 30,000 pairs of shoes per year, according to Gladwell, but then something fun-

ny happened. A few kids started wearing Hush Puppies to hip bars in New York, and the idea took off. In 1995, people bought 430,000 pairs of Hush Puppies. The next year they bought four times that number, all because a handful of kids thought they were cool.

PAYING IT FORWARD: CAN ACTS OF LOVE CHANGE THE WORLD?

As this book nears its close, I want to ask you: What if we could apply this theory to making our offices better, more loving places to work? What if every day each one of us committed an Act of Love that inspired others to be more loving? What if the people they touched also began to show more love in the workplace until we reached the tipping point? By committing to a few of the simple principles you've learned in this book, you can affect businesses and people's lives across the world.

Consider the following Acts of Love from one of our anonymous contributors and from Rod Canion. Incidentally, both have to do with the overwhelming gratitude one experiences when their boss gives them roadside assistance:

"I was working as a vice president of a technology-based call center based in truck-fleet roadside assistance. It was a privately owned company with about 500 employees.

"One of the agents on my team, who was a solid performer, could no longer make it in to work because her vehicle's transmission needed a complete replacement. She came to me and explained that she would likely need to resign since she no longer had transportation and no way to pay the amount a transmission would cost. She was quite distressed because not only did she love her job, but she also had a good income that she didn't believe she could get close to where she lived.

"I went to our president to explain the situation. He asked for the agent and me to come to his office that afternoon. At the meeting, our president said he would pay for the transmission replacement to keep the employee gainfully employed at our company.

"He also said the payback would not hurt since it would come directly from her paycheck as a small weekly deduction until it was fully paid. There would be no interest and no employment commitment. In other words, he took a leap of faith to help a frontline employee in distress.

"When I asked him why he would do this, he simply said, 'Do the right thing, do it right now.'"

— Anonymous

As I've mentioned, Rod was the co-founder of Compaq and a true influence on me as a young entrepreneur, when I was just getting Healthlink up and running. But how did Rod become a love-based leader, especially as the business world grew increasingly fear-based throughout his career?

"When I was a young engineer at Texas Instruments, around 1970, my two-year-old son, Scott, had an infection in the lymph node under his right jaw. The doctors had given him an antibiotic, but one evening when I was still at work, I got a call from my wife that his jaw had swollen. The doctor had told her to take him directly to Texas Children's Hospital (TCH) in Houston.

"We only had one car, so I needed to leave work immediately. My boss, Herman Pope, told me to go, but when I tried to start my car, the battery was dead. No one I asked had jumper cables, so Herman gave me his keys and told me to take his car.

"The doctors operated on my son to drain the infection, but it took TCH two more days to find the right antibiotic to cure him. Scott recovered, and to this day I remember the kindness that was showed to me."

— Rod Canion, founder, CEO, Compaq Computers

Think about this for a minute. As a young businessman in the 1970s, Rod experienced an Act of Love that made an impact on him. He started Compaq, a company that performed thousands of Acts of Love over time. Rod influenced me, and I went on to create thousands more Acts of Love through the many people who started at Healthlink and the other companies I've influenced. Now I have written this book that highlights Acts of Love that hopefully will reach thousands more people. It all started with a caring manager who just wanted to do a kind deed for his employee.

SHOWING ACTS OF KINDNESS TOWARD CUSTOMERS

All of the Acts of Love shared in this book have focused on the kindness and compassion shown by a boss to their employees. Acts of Love can also have a dramatic impact on the relationship between a business and its customers, as the following stories from Hamish Stewart-Smith, one of Encore's employees, and Darren Dworkin, one of Encore's customers, demonstrate:

"Part of earning the status of being 100% referenceable at Encore was to do the right thing if we ever got into the ditch with a client. Dana would always say that while we tried to be perfect, we may stub our toe now and again, and if that happened, we would do whatever it took to regain the client's trust and respect. The key was to have the people closest to the client figure out what to do to regain that trust.

"I got to see this in action on my first assignment. We had won a major project to help a large, 24-hospital system implement electronic medical records. It was complex work, and we had a large team on the ground. We hit a critical point for which we needed a high-caliber subject-matter expert to get us through.

"We interviewed and brought on a person who seemed like a perfect fit, but we got a sinking feeling after about two weeks that she was out of her depth. She was trying hard, but could not grasp the magnitude of the work or chart a course though it. We coached her as best we could, but after another week or so, it became obvious she couldn't succeed.

"I called my new team leader and explained the situation with not a little dread. He listened carefully, and then asked one question: 'What's the right thing to do?'

"I paused and said I should proactively go to the system CIO, explain the problem, show how we would protect the timeline, offer a free transition to another person, and repay the roughly $30,000 in fees already charged.

"My team leader said, 'Agreed, go do it.'

"The CIO was clearly pleasantly surprised by our discussion. He said he had never had a consulting firm do this, and he was very pleased he didn't have to find out about the problem himself. I know it went a long way toward building trust between us, and we went on to do hundreds of thousands of dollars of work together.

"Even more important was the impact this interaction had on me as one of the ground troops who had to fight these battles each day. In this business, we are only as good as our reputations, and my greatest fear was letting a customer down because my company didn't want to get it right. Knowing that I worked for a company that empowered me to make decisions based on doing 'the right thing' made me proud to work for Encore and motivated me to bring on the best and the brightest talent in the industry who all wanted to work in this kind of environment."

— Hamish Stewart-Smith, former Encore employee

Darren Dworkin is one of the top CIOs in the healthcare industry, managing Cedars-Sinai Medical Center, the prestigious and highly complex health system in Los Angeles, California. His story illustrates the impact of melding two cultures on a project that was critical to Cedars.

"By the time I really got to know Ivo and Dana, they had already successfully built, grown, and sold Healthlink to IBM. I was a first-time CIO trying to navigate my way in the complex world of healthcare IT delivery, and their reputations and those of their team were legendary. At Cedars-Sinai, we were doing the traditional consultant thing with one of the big firms and were ready to take a fresh look at something new. I was in luck: Encore had just launched.

"I remember our initial meeting well. A room of decision makers at Cedars-Sinai, including the CFO, CNO, and many others—a full alphabet soup of the C-suite—were being pitched by all the big firms. Then Ivo and Dana and their team came in. We introduced ourselves, had the usual chitchat, but then something weird happened. They didn't talk much. They asked questions, and, wait for it, they listened. They were a small firm we could all feel was poised to grow, but they wanted to know how they could help us build something first. It wouldn't be for them, built for their company's portfolio; instead, they wanted to know how they could help us build our own teams. Among their first priorities were to help us fill our open positions. They had our attention.

"I wouldn't come to really understand what made us bet on Encore and keep betting on them for years, but eventually the secret became clear: Ivo and Dana's love-based culture wasn't just about their teams, it also had a way of infiltrating, then influencing, and ultimately helping to change our own culture to be more like theirs. This was not because we had to, but because we came to want to. They understood that if you created a company that felt like a family, then over time customers like us would feel like an extension of that family.

"We would go on to launch a series of highly complex projects with great success with Encore by our side. We enjoyed their magical blend of love and unrivaled commitment to execution.

"But let's go back to that conference room, to when we were interviewing Encore. At the end of their presentation, our CFO said, 'So tell me why we should hire your company.'

"The room fell quiet for what felt like a really long time. Then Ivo's voice declared in his Texan drawl, ''Cause we'll get 'er done.'

"When phrases like this were uttered, it didn't mean everyone had to work double-time. It meant Ivo, Dana, and their team would figure out, regardless of any barrier, how to help us all win. They always found ways to partner with us to work past obstacles, not in scope but in what needed to be solved. We learned 'Get 'er done' was a way of saying, 'We have your back. We are your partner, no matter what it takes.' We had never seen anything like it—a vendor showing us love."

— Darren Dworkin, senior vice president of enterprise information services and chief information officer, Cedars-Sinai Medical Center

SMALL ACTS OF KINDNESS CAN BE HUGE

We can raise the consciousness of an entire company by raising the bar ourselves. At Healthlink, we had an unwritten practice that if you got upgraded to first class on a flight, you would give that ticket to the lowest-paid employee on the plane.

We frequently attended conferences and other events with admins and event planners. It was inspiring to see the looks on these employees' faces when the CEO or COO gave his or her first-class ticket to them. Most had never flown first-class before, and this gesture was a great message to them: They were as important as anyone else in the company. They were loved equally. All of our executives shared this practice. Giving up your first-class seat wasn't written into any policy manual. It was just our small way of saying thank you.

I later witnessed an airport scene that broke my heart with joy. I saw an old grandmother, likely in her 80s, use her cane to walk up to a man dressed in his military fatigues. She offered him her first-class seat to thank him for his service. He smiled graciously and didn't take her up on her offer, but to think that she would show such respect blew me away.

She showed him an Act of Love.

PRINCIPLE #10
ACTS OF LOVE
Show That You Care

The simplest, most profound action that a company can take toward a Love-Based Culture is to perform Acts of Love. This might be as simple as saying thank you to an employee who has put in some extra effort. It might involve attending an employee's parent's funeral or allowing a single mom to stay home with her sick child. The memory an employee will take away from any employer who performs Acts of Love is that he or she "cares about me."

Call to Action:

» Do you feel that openly caring about your employees and their families is encouraged at your company?

» If you're in a leadership position, would you be able to attend your employee's family member's funeral and be reimbursed for your travel by your employer?

» How can you share an Act of Love at your place of work tomorrow?

My Lessons Learned:

» The biggest mistakes I've made in my career are when I showed a lack of respect for a company's culture. Committing to a love-based culture means you are submitting to that culture. It's a marriage where divorce is NOT an option.

» Of all the Acts of Love I collected for this book, the one act that stood out beyond all others was when a boss attended a funeral. This is low-hanging fruit that tells your employee they mean the world to you and your company. This is a single day, at most, of your time. Love-based companies will make this a management policy, if it isn't already, and all travel will be reimbursed.

» Some companies try to automate their Acts of Love by allowing you to go online and punch a button that sends a message or a small gift to someone. While this act might be better than nothing, there really is nothing that replaces a personal touch. Acts of Love are done with people directly, not through a computer.

11

A FINAL CALL TO ACTION

You've read through *Love-Based Culture*, learned to identify 10 principles, and mastered the difference between leading with love and leading with fear.

So, you might be asking yourself, "Now what?" How can you make an impact in your organization that moves the needle toward love? It's simple. Below are five initiatives that will help you make an impact, no matter where you are in your company or your career.

1. START WITH YOU!

No matter where or how you work, whether you are a CEO, a manager, or an employee of a small, medium, or large; public or private; for-profit or nonprofit organization, if you want to work in a love-based culture, then my first piece of advice is to start with YOU.

I recently hosted a two-day retreat for a group of CEOs at my house. The purpose of retreats like this one is to give busy people the chance to recharge their batteries and share their personal and professional challenges in a safe environment. At the beginning of this particular retreat, I asked each of my guests to share with me any thoughts they had about their peers.

There was one CEO whose 360-degree feedback is relevant to my point. Prior to the retreat, everyone perceived him to be confident and strong, but also cocky, arrogant, superficial, and self-centered. After the retreat, though, the words that described him were "very human," approachable, caring, and thoughtful.

In other words, unless you grew close to this loving man, you really didn't know him. His years of training to be tough had painted a veneer on top of a person who was truly caring. On our retreat, I finally saw the side of him that most never experienced, the vulnerable side that needed to emerge so that he could fully realize what a great leader he could be.

Sometimes, supposed career mentors encourage people to present themselves differently on the outside than they are on the inside, usually in an effort to be "tough." Does being transparent and authentic make us look weak? Of course not. It's these traits that make us "real" and, ultimately, when paired with a natural desire to give more than we take, trustworthy. It's trust that is at the heart of a love-based culture. Without trust, none of the 10 principles of a love-based culture will work in the long term.

Regardless of where you fit in your company, the single emotion that forces the shields to go up is fear. This feeling of fear is real and sometimes necessary when the crisis of the day or hungry competitors are breathing down your neck, but when fear becomes pervasive and never goes away, then it becomes toxic. This is the fear that destroys people, the fear that creates cultures where CEOs can hide fraud and where short-term metrics take priority over the long-term viability of a company. Bad leaders rule with fear, frequently because they are too insecure to allow their vulnerabilities to be exposed, and by setting a poor example, bad leaders spawn more bad leaders.

> Perform Acts of Love for people who manage with fear so that they, too, can experience the impact of kindness at work.

2. SET A LOFTY GOAL THAT IS TOTALLY FOCUSED ON YOUR CLIENTS

It becomes infinitely more difficult to foster a love-based culture when your company is losing customers, laying off workers, and creating a feeling that you're playing defense in business. When fear-based companies start losing customers, they dig even deeper into their fear, with leaders looking for heads to chop and workers pointing fingers at everyone except themselves. (After all, who wants to lose their head?)

While many people reading this book will argue that employees should come first, the fact is that the biggest single risk to a company's culture is when the company stops growing and gaining new customers. A company's safety and survival will always take precedence over love for the individual employee when the company is at risk. Create a culture where letting even one customer down is unacceptable, where there are no rationalizations for failure, and where acquiring and retaining customers is owned by everyone from the CEO to the receptionist, and it's likely your company will grow. When it does, your employees will be more likely to move from fear and survival mode to a positive, loving environment and feel like winners.

> **Perform Acts of Love for employees who go above and beyond to keep your company 100% referenceable.**

3. IT'S THE SOFT SIDE OF BUSINESS THAT TOUCHES THE HEART

People want to work for a company with values and goals that resonate with their own personal beliefs, where coming to work feels so natural that they don't have to be a different person than they are at home.

Know the core values of your organization and integrate them into your daily work life. Encourage your company to take what currently may be a document hanging on the wall in the conference room and turn it into a living document that is actively discussed in team meetings. Take time to discuss each value, including when people in your organization supported or didn't support that value. If a value wasn't respected, discuss how you could have done better as a team. Be transparent in your meetings, using these discussions as an opportunity not only to improve, but also as a way to increase employee awareness of that value. Do this, and each value will come alive.

Moreover, understand your organization's higher calling. Create a focus around that calling, and engage in activities that support it. Everyone wants to be a part of something bigger, to go beyond enhancing shareholder equity. We all have a higher calling that our organizations can tap into and use to create meaning for our employees. This higher calling will pull them together to achieve goals that make them proud of the organization for which they work.

> Perform Acts of Love for people who exemplify the values of your company and strive for your higher calling.

4. EMPOWER EMPLOYEES WHO ARE CLOSE TO CUSTOMERS TO MAKE DECISIONS

An underlying tenet of a love-based culture is to trust the people in your organization to do what's right—that is, to make decisions that are in the best interest of the organization without handholding or micromanagement. This is key if you set your quality standard at having 100% customer referenceability. Customer-facing employees need to be empowered to solve problems while in the heat of battle without having to go through long, bureaucratic permission processes. At the same time, boundaries for these decisions need to be created and communicated so that your company is not put at extreme risk.

In the event that a poor decision is made, it should be viewed as a learning opportunity. Fear-based companies discipline their employees for poor decisions, thus eliminating any chance for others to learn from the mistake. They create a culture where there is a lack of transparency, which only serves to hide errors and increase internal pain. While quick demand decisions from employees may cost your organization money in the short term, the benefit of having happy customers and a culture that feels empowered to solve problems quickly far outweighs the costs.

> Perform Acts of Love for people who have made bold decisions to solve big problems for your customers.

5. SUPPORT YOUR CULTURE WITH POLICIES AND PROCEDURES THAT SHOW YOU TRUST AND VALUE YOUR EMPLOYEES

While there are policies and procedures that are required by regulatory agencies or the government, design your company's response to most of them with an assumption that your employees can be trusted. Creating policies and procedures that penalize 99% of your organization for something they haven't done will ultimately cost you more money and increase the costs of administration.

A love-based culture trusts its people to spend the organization's money like it's their own. Showing flexibility around expense reporting, vacation days, sick leave, and other required policies will help create a culture where people adhere to policies because of the respect you've shown them rather than because they fear the implications of non-compliance.

Compensation should be based first on your organization's success at meeting its goals. Based on the level of success achieved, each person in the organization should be compensated based on their role in helping to create that success.

While employees have individual metrics to help define their goals, it's to be understood that there is more to performance than what can be measured. A person's ability to lift their team to a higher level, their ability to bring in new A+ players to grow the company, and their flexibility in pivoting to solve problems without being asked are all characteristics of those we think of as being our best people.

> Perform Acts of Love that recognize the unique needs of each employee, whether it is allowing for flexibility with paid time off, sick days, or other personal issues, or if it is giving recognition to a superstar.

There is a special feeling that emerges when each of these elements is implemented actively and successfully. When this happens, everyone feels like a winner. When you are living in a fear-based culture, failure destroys people and success becomes bittersweet. The move to a love-based culture creates an environment where winning isn't defined by your own individual success, but by the joy and ecstasy you feel in watching your team and your peers succeed.

THE CIRCLE OF LOVE

I live in a rural town north of Houston, Texas, called Huntsville. Our town is mostly known for having five prisons and Sam Houston State University, but I'm here because of family.

My wife and I live on a little lake on the edge of Sam Houston National Forest. My 92-year-old father lives right next door. My older sister and her husband live next door to him, and across the street is my younger sister and her husband, a constantly changing number of dogs and cats, and a brood of chickens, the eggs from which I rarely see. My son lives down the street.

When we're all in town at the same time, we will convene for a group dinner. We assemble in what I've coined "The Circle of Love," in which we stand in a circle holding hands as my dad shares a prayer that always includes the word "forgiveness."

Though the feelings I have for those in our Circle of Love are different from the feelings I have for the many people with whom I've worked over the decades, there is a common thread. While we didn't stand around every morning in the Healthlink lobby in Circles of Love, we still genuinely cared about one another.

We were on a mission to build a great company and felt a higher calling. We had each other's backs when one of us fell and needed help getting up. We all felt the pain when a family member was sick or a parent was at the end of their life. And we all knew, deep in our hearts, that our customers were the only ones who could measure our success. It took all of us working together as a team to make them happy.

While many people care about launching their careers to even greater heights, there is an emerging population of workers who also care about contributing to the greater good. Today's employees raise the bar because they care. When you combine these powerful forces into personal missions, ones on which team members can find abundance both financially and in a purpose at work, your company will become more than just another business. Your company will become a part of a movement that makes a difference.

Let's get going; we've got a lot of love to do.

10 PRINCIPLES OF A LOVE-BASED CULTURE

100% Referenceability

Become obsessed with a bold, customer-centered goal.
My company has a goal of 100% customer satisfaction. We would have no business without clients who believe in my company because of our outstanding products and services.

Leadership

Put your employees' needs ahead of your own.
The executives at my company put their employees' needs above their own. I trust the leadership of my company. They care about me.

Core Values

Be uncompromising in living core values daily.
I know, understand, and feel ownership of my company's core values. The executives at my company "walk the talk." I feel safe working for my company.

A Higher Calling

Have purpose beyond profits.
I believe my company is passionate about how we contribute to the greater good of society. I can pursue a higher calling by working at my company.

Governance

Focus on long-term growth.

My company's board of directors holds executives accountable for the long-term success of the company, not for meeting short-term financial goals. The directors are not at risk of being surprised due to a lack of transparency in my company.

Compensation

Reward those who add value.

My compensation is based on my company's success and on the overall value I provide in contributing to that success. It is not solely metrics-driven. I trust my manager to pay me fairly. My company rewards an employee's value to the company regardless of their success in achieving their individual performance goals.

Winning

Feel the buzz of success.

My company makes me feel like a winner because of the overwhelming positive energy I feel every day when I come to work. I work hard because I want to make my company successful.

The 3 Ps: Policies, Processes, Performance

Hardwire processes to trust.

The policies in my company are based on trust rather than on penalties. The processes in my company support teamwork. My manager and I have productive, two-way, honest, and candid conversations about my performance.

Decision-Making

Empower those closest to the customer to do what's right.

The managers of my company are empowered to make decisions (within predetermined boundaries) that impact customers. I feel trusted to show good judgment to solve problems without asking for permission.

Acts of Love

Show that you care.

The executives of my company perform acts of love for their team. As an employee, I have benefited from acts of kindness.

NOTES

Introduction

1. Wartzman, Rick, and Lawrence Crosby. "A Company's Performance Depends First of All on Its People." *The Wall Street Journal*. August 12, 2018. www.wsj.com/articles/a-companys-performance-depends-first-of-all-on-its-people-1534125840.

2. Fuhrmans, Vanessa, and Yoree Koh. "The 250 Most Effectively Managed U.S. Companies—and How They Got That Way." *Wall Street Journal*. December 6, 2017. www.wsj.com/articles/the-most-effectively-managed-u-s-companiesand-how-they-got-that-way-1512482887.

3. Ibid.

4. Wartzman, Rick, and Lawrence Crosby. "A Company's Performance Depends First of All on Its People." *The Wall Street Journal*. August 12, 2018. www.wsj.com/articles/a-companys-performance-depends-first-of-all-on-its-people-1534125840.

5. Edmans, Alex. "Why Happier Workers Matter More than You Think." World Economic Forum. January 6, 2015. www.weforum.org/agenda/2015/01/why-happier-workers-matter/.

6. Levering, Robert, and Milton Moskowitz. "100 Best Companies to Work for in America 1984." Great Place to Work Institute. 2018. www.greatplacetowork.net/bestworkplaces/a2480000005kCEP.

7. Edmans, Alex. "Why Happier Workers Matter More than You Think." World Economic Forum. January 6, 2015. www.weforum.org/agenda/2015/01/why-happier-workers-matter/.

8. Bush, Michael, and Sarah Lewis-Kulin. "Here's How to Get on Our Best Companies to Work For List." *Fortune*. March 9, 2017. http://fortune.com/2017/03/09/best-companies-list-how-to/.

Chapter 1

1. "Vision 2020." Volvo Cars. Accessed 2019. www.volvocars.com/en-ca/about/our-stories/vision-2020.

Chapter 2

1. Curtin, Melanie. "In Just 10 Words, This Former CEO of a Billion-Dollar Company Explains the Purpose of Life." *Inc.* September 18, 2018. www.inc.com/melanie-curtin/in-just-10-words-this-former-ceo-of-a-billion-dollar-company-explains-purpose-of-life.html.

2. Schwantes, Marcel. "Warren Buffet Says Your Greatest Measure of Success at the End of Your Life Comes Down to One Word." *Inc.* September 13, 2018. www.inc.com/marcel-schwantes/warren-buffett-says-it-doesnt-matter-how-rich-you-are-without-this-1-thing-your-life-is-a-disaster.html.

3. Eurich, Tasha. "What Self-Awareness Really Is (and How to Cultivate It)." *Harvard Business Review.* January 4, 2018. https://hbr.org/2018/01/what-self-awareness-really-is-and-how-to-cultivate-it.

4. "IBM to Acquire Healthlink Incorporated, Nation's Foremost Healthcare Consulting Services Company." IBM News Release. April 26, 2005. https://www-03.ibm.com/press/us/en/pressrelease/7631.wss.

Chapter 3

1. "Gallup releases new insights on the state of the global workplace." Gallup. October 8, 2013. https://news.gallup.com/opinion/gallup/171632/gallup-releases-new-insights-state-global-work-place.aspx.

2. "The Five I's of Employee Engagement." *The American Business Journal.* December/January 2013. www.abjusa.com/features/features_dec_jan_13/the_five_i_s_of_employee_engagement.html.

3. Deci, Edward, and Richard M. Ryan. *Intrinsic Motivation and Self-Determination in Human Behavior.* Perspectives in Social Psychology Series. New York: Plenum Press, 1985.

4. Tews, Michael J., John W. Michel, and A. L. Bartlett. "The Fundamental Role of Workplace Fun in Applicant Attraction." *Journal of Leadership & Organizational Studies.* 19.1 (2012): 105–14. www.researchgate.net/publication/254116622_The_Fundamental_Role_of_Workplace_Fun_in_Applicant_Attraction/download.

5. Gurchiek, Kathy. "Fun at Work Fundamental: Study." Society for Human Resource Develop- ment. September 24, 2012. https://www.shrm.org/resourcesandtools/hr-topics/organizational-and-employee-development/pages/fun-at-work-study.aspx.

6. Ibid.

Chapter 4

1. "Conscious Capitalism." Conscious Capitalism, *Inc.* 2019. https://www.consciouscapitalism.org/

2. Mackey, John, and Rajendra Sisodia. Conscious Capitalism: *Liberating the Heroic Spirit of Business*. Cambridge, MA: Harvard Business Review Press, 2014.

3. *Culture of Purpose: A Business Imperative. 2013 Core Beliefs & Culture Survey*. Deloitte LLP. 2013. https://docplayer.net/11003057-Culture-of-purpose-a-business-imperative-2013-core-beliefs-culture-survey.html

4. Ibid.

5. Alton, Larry. "How Millennials are reshaping what's important in corporate culture." *Forbes*. June 20, 2017. www.forbes.com/sites/larryalton/2017/06/20/how-millennials-are-reshaping-whats-important-in-corporate-culture/#3ac3a0272dfb.

6. Crew, Jonathan. "Why Millennials Would Take a $7,600 Pay Cut for a New Job." *Fortune*. April 8, 2016. http://fortune.com/2016/04/08/fidelity-millennial-study-career/.

7. "Patagonia's Mission Statement." Patagonia. 2019. www.patagonia.com/company-info.html.

8. "Fighting Hunger, One Bowl of Soup at a Time." Panera Bread. 2018. www.panerabread.com/en-us/articles/fighting-hunger-a-bowl-of-soup-at-a-time-video.html.

9. "Our Mission." Honest Tea. 2019. www.honesttea.com/about-us/our-mission/.

10. "The Body Shop Approach to Stakeholder Auditing." Business Case Studies. 2019. http://businesscasestudies.co.uk/body-shop/the-body-shop-approach-to-stakeholder-auditing/introduction.html.

11. "Improving Lives." TOMS. 2019. www.toms.com/improving-lives.

12. "The TOMS Story." TOMS. 2019. www.toms.com/about-toms.

Chapter 5

1. "Employee Tenure Summary." U.S. Department of Labor - Bureau of Labor Statistics. September 20, 2018. www.bls.gov/news.release/tenure.nr0.htm.

2. Elmer, Vickie. "50-plus years on the job: An extremely rare bird." *Fortune*. February 28, 2014. http://fortune.com/2014/02/28/50-plus-years-on-the-job-an-extremely-rare-bird/.

3. Ibid.

4. Ibid.

5. Drucker, Peter F. *The Practice of Management*. New York: Harper Business, 2006. Reprint.

6. Wilson, Deborah, Bronwyn Croxson, and Adele Atkinson. "What Gets Measured Gets Done." *Policy Studies*. 27 (2): 153–71. Published online August 22, 2006. www.tandfonline.com/doi/abs/10.1080/01442870600637995.

7. Musk, Elon. "Taking Tesla Private." Tesla. August 7, 2018. www.tesla.com/BLOG/taking-tesla-Private.

8. De la Merced, Michael J., and Matt Phillips. "Trump Asks S.E.C. to Study Quarterly Earnings Requirements for Public Firms." *New York Times*. August 17, 2018. www.nytimes.com/2018/08/17/business/dealbook/trump-quarterly-earnings.html.

Chapter 7

1. Sun Tzu. *The Art of War*. Trans. Lionel Giles. St. Augustine, Florida: Greyhound Press, 2017.

2. Ibid.

3. Goh, Joel, Jeffery Pfeffer, and Stefanos A. Zenios. "Workplace Stressors and Health Outcomes: Health Policy for the Workplace." *Behavioral Science & Policy*. Spring 2015. 1(1): 43-52. www.hbs.edu/faculty/ Pages/item.aspx?num=50306.

4. White, Gillian B. "The Alarming, Long-Term Consequences of Workplace Stress." *The Atlantic*. February 12, 2015. www.theatlantic.com/business/archive/2015/02/the-alarming-long- term-consequences-of-workplace-stress/385397/.

5. Ibid.

6. Lynch, Shana. "Why Your Workplace Might be Killing You." Insights by Stanford Business. February 23, 2015. www.gsb.stanford.edu/insights/why-your-workplace-might-be-killing-you.

7. Nguyen, Steve, Ph.D. "Cost of Stress on the U.S. Economy is $300 Billion? Says Who?" *Workplace Psychology*. July 4, 2016. https://workplacepsychology.net/2016/07/04/cost-of-stress-on- the-u-s-economy-is-300-billion-says-who/.

8. "Research Finds Stress is Bad for Workers, Bad for Business." SFM Mutual Insurance Company. April 18, 2017. www.sfmic.com/work-stress-research/.

9. Curtin, Melanie. "In Just 10 Words, This Former CEO of a Billion-Dollar Company Explains the Purpose of Life." *Inc*. September 18, 2018. www.inc.com/melanie-curtin/ in-just-10-words-this-former-ceo-of-a-billion-dollar-company-explains-purpose-of-life.html.

10. Williams, David K. "Forgiveness: The Least Understood Leadership Trait in the Workplace." *Forbes*. January 5, 2015. www.forbes.com/sites/davidkwilliams/2015/01/05/forgiveness-the-least-understood-leadership-trait-in-the-workplace-2/#2a862c86b3f2.

11. Bushak, Lecia. "How Forgiveness Benefits Your Health: Forgiving Wrongdoers Can Expand Physical Fitness." *Medical Daily*. January 7, 2015. www.medicaldaily.com/ how-forgiveness-benefits-your-health-forgiving-wrongdoers-can-expand-physical-fitness-316902.

Chapter 8

1. Detert, James R., and Amy C. Edmonson. "Why Employees are Afraid to Speak." Harvard Business Review. May 2007. https://hbr.org/2007/05/why-employees-are-afraid-to-speak.

Chapter 9

1. "There's a .00006% Chance of Building a Billion-Dollar Company: How This Man Did It." *First Round Review*. September 24, 2018. http://firstround.com/review/Theres-a-00006-Chance- of-Building-a-Billion-Dollar-Company-How-This-Man-Did-It/.

2. Detert, James R., and Amy C. Edmondson. "Why Employees Are Afraid to Speak." *Harvard Business Review*. May 2007. https://hbr.org/2007/05/why-employees-are-afraid-to-speak.

3. Gerstner, Jr., Louis V. *Who Says Elephants Can't Dance?* New York: Harper Business, 2002.

4. Gharib, Susie. "Martin Marietta CEO Says Strong Values are the Key to Great Leadership." *Fortune*. April 17, 2018. http://fortune.com/2018/04/17/martin-marietta-ward-nye-leadership/.

5. Connley, Courtney. "Why Marc Benioff Makes Salesforce Employees Do Volunteer Work on Their First Day. CNBC. June 28, 2018. www.cnbc.com/2018/06/27/why-marc-benioff-makes-salesforce-employees-do-this-on-their-first-day.html.

6. Chamberlain, Andrew. "Beating the Market Again: Updated Stock Returns for Best Places to Work Companies." Glassdoor. December 8, 2015. www.glassdoor.com/research/2016-bptw-stock-returns/.

7. Cappelli, Peter, and Anna Tavis. "The Performance Management Revolution." *Harvard Business Review*. October 2016. https://hbr.org/2016/10/the-performance-management-revolution.

8. Medvec, Victoria, "When Should Leaders Own a Decision and When Should They Delegate?" *Kellogg Insight*. Accessed November 8, 2018. https://insight.kellogg.northwestern.edu/article/how-should-leaders-make-efficient-decisions.

9. Weller, Chris. "16 Accidental Inventions that Changed the World." *Business Insider*. June 22, 2016. www.businessinsider.com/accidental-inventions-that-changed-the-world-2016-6.

Chapter 10

1. Gladwell, Malcolm. *The Tipping Point*. New York: Little Brown, 2000.

BIBLIOGRAPHY

Alton, Larry. "How Millennials are Reshaping What's Important in Corporate Culture." *Forbes.* June 20, 2017. www.forbes.com/sites/larryalton/2017/06/20/how-millennials-are-reshaping-whats-important-in-corporate-culture/#3ac3a0272dfb

"The Body Shop Approach to Stakeholder Auditing." Business Case Studies. 2019. http://businesscasestudies.co.uk/body-shop/the-body-shop-approach-to-stakeholder-auditing/introduction.html

Bush, Michael, and Sarah Lewis-Kulin. "Here's How to Get on Our Best Companies to Work For List." *Fortune.* March 9, 2017. http://fortune.com/2017/03/09/best-companies-list-how-to/

Bushak, Lecia. "How Forgiveness Benefits Your Health: Forgiving Wrongdoers Can Expand Physical Fitness." *Medical Daily.* January 7, 2015. www.medicaldaily.com/how-forgiveness-benefits-your-health-forgiving-wrongdoers-can-expand-physical-fitness-316902

Cappelli, Peter, and Anna Tavis. "The Performance Management Revolution." *Harvard Business Review.* October 2016. https://hbr.org/2016/10/the-performance-management-revolution

Chamberlain, Andrew. "Beating the Market Again: Updated Stock Returns for Best Places to Work Companies." Glassdoor. December 8, 2015. www.glassdoor.com/research/2016-bptw-stock-returns/

Connley, Courtney. "Why Marc Benioff Makes Salesforce Employees Do Volunteer Work on Their First Day." CNBC. June 28, 2018. www.cnbc.com/2018/06/27/why-marc-benioff-makes-salesforce-employees-do-this-on-their-first-day.html

"Conscious Capitalism." Conscious Capitalism, Inc. 2019. https://www.consciouscapitalism.org/

Crew, Jonathan. "Why Millennials Would Take a $7,600 Pay Cut for a New Job." *Fortune.* April 8, 2016. http://fortune.com/2016/04/08/fidelity-millennial-study-career/

Culture of Purpose: A Business Imperative. 2013 Core Beliefs & Culture Survey. Deloitte LLP. 2013. https://docplayer.net/11003057-Culture-of-purpose-a-business-imperative-2013-core-beliefs-culture-survey.html

Curtin, Melanie. "In Just 10 Words, This Former CEO of a Billion-Dollar Company Explains the Purpose of Life." *Inc.* September 18, 2018. www.inc.com/melanie-curtin/in-just-10-words-this-former-ceo-of-a-billion-dollar-company-explains-purpose-of-life.html

De la Merced, Michael J., and Matt Phillips. "Trump Asks S.E.C. to Study Quarterly Earnings Requirements for Public Firms." *New York Times.* August 17, 2018. www.nytimes.com/2018/08/ 17/business/dealbook/trump-quarterly-earnings.html

Deci, Edward, and Richard M. Ryan. *Intrinsic Motivation and Self-Determination in Human Behavior.* Perspectives in Social Psychology Series. New York: Plenum Press, 1985.

Detert, James R., and Amy C. Edmonson. "Why Employees are Afraid to Speak." *Harvard Business Review.* May 2007. https://hbr.org/2007/05/why-employees-are-afraid-to-speak

Drucker, Peter F. *The Practice of Management.* New York: Harper Business, 2006.

Edmans, Alex. "Why Happier Workers Matter More than You Think." World Economic Forum. January 6, 2015. www.weforum.org/agenda/2015/01/why-happier-workers-matter/

Elmer, Vickie. "50-Plus Years on the Job: An Extremely Rare Bird." *Fortune.* February 28, 2014. http://fortune.com/2014/02/28/50-plus-years-on-the-job-an-extremely-rare-bird/

"Employee Tenure Summary." U.S. Department of Labor–Bureau of Labor Statistics. September 20, 2018. www.bls.gov/news.release/tenure.nr0.htm

Eurich, Tasha. "What Self-Awareness Really Is (and How to Cultivate It)." *Harvard Business Review.* January 4, 2018. https://hbr.org/2018/01/what-self-awareness-really-is-and-how-to-cultivate-it

"Fighting Hunger, One Bowl of Soup at a Time." Panera Bread. 2018. www.panerabread.com/en-us/articles/fighting-hunger-a-bowl-of-soup-at-a-time-video.html

"The Five I's of Employee Engagement." *The American Business Journal.* December/January 2013. www.abjusa.com/features/ features_dec_jan_13/the_five_i_s_of_employee_engagement.html

Fuhrmans, Vanessa, and Yoree Koh. "The 250 Most Effectively Managed U.S. Companies—and How They Got That Way." *Wall Street Journal.* December 6, 2017. www.wsj.com/articles/the-most-effectively-managed-u-s-companiesand-how-they-got-that-way-1512482887

"Gallup Releases New Insights on the State of the Global Workplace." Gallup, Inc. October 8, 2013. https://news.gallup.com/opinion/gallup/171632/gallup-releases-new-insights-state-global-workplace.aspx

Gerstner, Jr., Louis V. *Who Says Elephants Can't Dance?* New York: Harper Business, 2002.

Gharib, Susie. "Martin Marietta CEO Says Strong Values are the Key to Great Leadership." *Fortune.* April 17, 2018. http://fortune.com/2018/04/17/martin-marietta-ward-nye-leadership/

Gladwell, Malcolm. *The Tipping Point.* New York: Little Brown, 2000.

Goh, Joel, Jeffery Pfeffer, and Stefanos A. Zenios. "Workplace Stressors and Health Outcomes: Health Policy for the Workplace." *Behavioral Science & Policy.* 2015. 1(1): 43-52. www.hbs.edu/faculty/Pages/item.aspx?num=50306

Gurchiek, Kathy. "Fun at Work Fundamental: Study." Society for Human Resource Management. September 24, 2012. www.shrm.org/resourcesandtools/hr-topics/organizational-and-employee-development/pages/fun-at-work-study.aspx

"IBM to Acquire Healthlink Incorporated, Nation's Foremost Healthcare Consulting Services Company." IBM. April 26, 2005. www-03.ibm.com/press/us/en/pressrelease/7631.wss

"Improving Lives." Toms. 2019. www.toms.com/improving-lives

Levering, Robert, and Milton Moskowitz. "100 Best Companies to Work for in America 1984." Great Place to Work Institute. 2018. www.greatplacetowork.net/bestworkplaces/a2480000005kCEP

Lynch, Shana. "Why Your Workplace Might be Killing You." *Insights by Stanford Business.* Stanford Graduate School of Business. February 23, 2015. www.gsb.stanford.edu/insights/why-your-workplace-might-be-killing-you

Mackey, John, and Rajendra Sisodia. *Conscious Capitalism: Liberating the Heroic Spirit of Business.* Cambridge, MA: Harvard Business Review Press, 2014

Medvec, Victoria. "When Should Leaders Own a Decision and When Should They Delegate?" *Kellog Insight.* Accessed November 8, 2018. https://insight.kellogg.northwestern.edu/ article/how-should-leaders-make-efficient-decisions

Nguyen, Steve, Ph.D. "Cost of Stress on the U.S. Economy is $300 billion? Says Who?" *Workplace Psychology.* July 4, 2016. https://workplacepsychology.net/2016/07/04/cost-of-stress-on-the-u-s- economy-is-300-billion-says-who/

"Our Mission." Honest Tea. 2019. www.honesttea.com/about-us/our-mission/

"Patagonia's Mission Statement." Patagonia. 2019. www.patagonia.com/company-info.html

"Research Finds That Stress Is Bad For Workers, Bad For Business." SFM Mutual Insurance Company. April 18, 2017. www.sfmic.com/work-stress-research/

Schwantes, Marcel. "Warren Buffet Says Your Greatest Measure of Success at the End of Your Life Comes Down to One Word." *Inc.* September 13, 2018. www.inc.com/marcel-schwantes/warren-buffett-says-it-doesnt-matter-how-rich-you-are-without-this-1-thing-your-life-is-a-disaster.html

Sun Tzu. *The Art of War.* Trans. Lionel Giles. St. Augustine, Florida: Greyhound Press, 2017.

Tews, Michael J., John W. Michel, and A. L. Bartlett. "The Fundamental Role of Workplace Fun in Applicant Attraction." *Journal of Leadership & Organizational Studies.* January 2012. 19(1):105–14. www.researchgate.net/publication/ 254116622_The_Fundamental_Role_of_ Workplace_Fun_in_ Applicant_Attraction/download

"There's a .00006% Chance of Building a Billion-Dollar Company: How This Man Did It." *First Round Review.* September 24, 2018. https://firstround.com/review/Theres-a-00006-Chance-of-Building-a-Billion-Dollar-Company-How-This-Man-Did-It/

"The TOMS Story." Toms. 2019. www.toms.com/about-toms.

"Vision 2020." Volvo Cars. Accessed 2019. www.volvocars.com/en-ca/about/our-stories/vision-2020

Wartzman, Rick, and Lawrence Crosby. "A Company's Performance Depends First of All on Its People," *The Wall Street Journal.* August 12, 2018. www.wsj.com/articles/a-companys-per-formance-depends-first-of-all-on-its-people-1534125840

Weller, Chris. "16 Accidental Inventions That Changed the World." *Business Insider.* June 22, 2016. www.businessinsider.com/accidental-inventions-that-changed-the-world-2016-6

White, Gillian B. "The Alarming, Long-Term Consequences of Workplace Stress." *The Atlantic.* February 12, 2015. www.theatlantic.com/business/archive/2015/02/the-alarming-long-term-consequences-of-workplace-stress/385397/

Williams, David K. "Forgiveness: The Least Understood Leadership Trait in the Workplace." *Forbes.* January 5, 2015. www.forbes.com/sites/davidkwilliams/2015/01/05/forgiveness-the-least-understood-leadership-trait-in-the-workplace-2/#2a862c86b3f2

Wilson, Deborah, Bronwyn Croxson, and Adele Atkinson. "What Gets Measured Gets Done." Policy Studies. 27(2): 153–71. Published August 22, 2006. www.tandfonline.com/doi/ abs/10.1080/01442870600637995

The Love-Based Team
Who Made It Happen

Calli Dretke – *Master of the Universe*
https://www.nextwaveconnect.com/

Jessica Hatch – *The Editor Who Makes Ivo Sound Good*
https://hatch-books.com/

Becky Bayne – *The Designer Who Makes Ivo Look Good*
https://beckysgraphicdesign.com/

The Love-Based Contributors Who Provided Real-World Advice

Chris Belmont
Bettyann Bird
Jeff Blanchard
Joe Boyd
Juliet Breeze, M.D.
George Brinkle
Beth Brown
Ken Bugh
Rod Canion
Laura Caperton
Tom Caperton
Bruce Cerullo
Charles (Chuck) Christian
Melanie C-J
Tiffani Clark
Tom Cocozza
James Coffin
George S. Conklin
Deidre Crippens Graham
Michael Davis
Darren Dworkin
Lesley Elliott
Chuck Emery
Butch Evans
Emily Evans
Cherrill Farnsworth
Steve Favaloro
David Greenwalt
John Gribi
Eve-Anne Grynsztajn
Donna Hadden

Becky Heflin
Patricia Holmes
Zac Jiwa
Lise Kifer
Karen Knecht
Bryna Kranzler
David Matuszak
Cathy Menkiena
Patty McCabe-Remmell
Tom Miller
Corbie Mitleid
Bill Montgomery
Keith Moody
Lisa Morlaes
Pete Morse
Paul Murphy
Wendy Lee Nentwig
Deb Niemeyer
Randy Osteen
Stephen Passalacqua
Charles Riley
Twila Ross
Bev Sninchak
Cheryl Stavins
Hamish Stewart-Smith
Teri Thomas
Joe Zelcovich
and Buckly, DJ,
King, Bella, Honey,
Coon, Koda, Mabel

If I neglected to include someone who helped me write the book, then please write your name here: _____

Many thanks to Tammy Kling and Tiarra Tompkins with OnFire Books for helping me to get started on this project and for sticking with me through all the pivots.

IVO NELSON was an early proponent of clinical transformation through technology, which helped his company Healthlink become the world's largest privately held, provider-focused healthcare technology consulting firm before its acquisition by IBM in 2005. He has participated as an advisor, investor, and CEO in more than nine start-ups, including Next Wave Connect, Next Wave Health Advisors, and Encore. He has sat on more than 20 boards, including the boards of Global HealthCare Alliance, Encore Health Resources, and HealthPost. Ivo was named one of the top 50 contributors to the healthcare IT industry by HIMSS; has received the prestigious Ernst & Young Entrepreneur of the Year Award; and was the first recipient of the University of Texas Health John P. Glaser Health Informatics Innovator Award. Recently, he founded IVO, an organization focused not only on enabling authentic and caring business leaders, but also on establishing a foundation for innovation, measured risk-taking, profitability, and growth.

DANA SELLERS served as president and chief operating officer of Healthlink, as well as founder and chief executive officer of Encore, one of *Modern Healthcare's* "Best Places to Work in Healthcare." Over a career spanning more than 40 years in healthcare technology and consulting, Dana has helped healthcare providers across the country bring about positive change through improved processes, enabling technology, and the insights that come from business intelligence and health analytics.

WANT TO KEEP THE CONVERSATION GOING?
Join the Movement!

I believe that most leaders have been brainwashed into believing that showing love in the workplace is a sign of weakness. The reality is that being open, transparent, and authentic requires a level of self-awareness that most business leaders lack.

I've built and grown companies, and I know how hard it can be to thrive in the heat of competition. I believe that the companies that win have love-based leaders at every level. Love-based leaders help serve customers that become repeat clients and sources of referral business. They hire and manage employees who stay for years, if not decades, and who feel proud to go to work everyday.

To help you hit these benchmarks, I founded IVO, an organization designed to help businesses grow by building healthy cultures with authentic leadership. At IVO, we're creating a movement that activates its mission through inspiration, education, and application.

» **INSPIRATION.** We provoke leaders to think deeply about what matters and to aspire to new heights. Visit the Acts of Love website at www.actsoflove.com to read inspiring stories of personal struggles and triumphs, kindness and compassion, or to share your own Act of Love with the world.

» **EDUCATION.** We equip leaders with the skills necessary to bridge knowledge and action. To help you connect with your community and find the right content to create profound change in your teams and organizations, we have launched myIVO. This social networking site is filled with videos, podcasts, articles, and communities devoted to creating open lines of communication among today's business leaders. To create your free profile and begin connecting, visit www.myivo.org.

» **APPLICATION.** We provide the means for leaders to position, advocate for, and utilize the Love-Based Culture framework within their organizations. In addition to the resources available on myIVO, leaders can connect directly with me and register their organization through www.ivo. com to receive Love-Based Culture study guides and worksheets to share with their teams.

CPSIA information can be obtained
at www.ICGtesting.com
Printed in the USA
FSHW011920070419
57024FS

9 781733 763202